OLD TESTAMENT CHALLENGE 1

CREATING A NEW COMMUNITY

OLD TESTAMENT CHALLENGE 1

CREATING A NEW COMMUNITY

LIFE-CHANGING STORIES FROM THE PENTATEUCH

JOHN ORTBERG

WITH KEVIN & SHERRY HARNEY

ZONDERVAN™

GRAND RAPIDS, MICHIGAN 49530 USA

WILLOW CREEK RESOURCES

ZONDERVAN™

Old Testament Challenge Volume 1: Creating a New Community Teaching Guide
Copyright © 2003 by Willow Creek Association

Requests for information should be addressed to:

Zondervan, *Grand Rapids, Michigan 49530*

ISBN 0-310-24892-2

Interior design by Sharon VanLoozenoord

Interior composition by Beth Shagene

Printed in the United States of America

03 04 05 06 07 08 09 /❖ ML/ 10 9 8 7 6 5 4 3 2

CONTENTS

intr⊙ducti⊙n

The Old Testament Challenge (OTC) is designed to foster spiritual formation and growth on three distinct levels (congregation-wide, small group, and individual). The first level of learning is with the full community of God's people. This teaching resource can be used in the setting of a worship service or in a large class. The primary reason these materials were developed was for use in a worship service, but there could also be some application of these materials in a larger class setting.

This teaching resource is designed to give teachers a wealth of ideas as they prepare to bring a message from God's Word. These materials have been designed to provide a large pool of information on the text and ideas for preaching. From these materials, the teacher can shape and form a message that fits the congregation he or she serves. As you will discover when you begin to dig into the teaching resources, there are far more source materials and ideas than can be incorporated in a normal sermon or teaching session. Each teacher will need to decide what materials best fit their situation, add their own personal illustrations and teaching ideas, and then form a message that fits their congregation and personal teaching style.

These materials have intentionally been developed on two levels. First, John Ortberg wrote the initial messages and preached them at Willow Creek Community Church. John developed these messages to teach them at the New Community Believer's Services. You will find an audiotape or CD of these messages in each of the four OTC kits. You will also notice that there were a few guest preachers who took part in the OTC teaching at Willow Creek.

Next, the materials and resources from the OTC were then adapted for a second-generation OTC church, Corinth Church in Grand Rapids, Michigan. Kevin Harney continued the process of developing and expanding the materials as he preached the messages in the Sunday morning services at Corinth Church. New illustrations, creative message ideas, Power Point presentations, Frequently Asked Questions about the Old Testament, and other study materials were added and the messages were expanded. Although John Ortberg was the primary writer/teacher at Willow Creek and Kevin Harney the primary writer/teacher at Corinth Church, a whole team of teachers, leaders, and editors have partnered together to develop and create this teaching resource.

What makes the teaching resource for the OTC so unique are the many different tools offered to the teacher in this Old Testament Challenge kit. When you open the teacher's resource, you will find the following categories of material in various combinations:

- Creative Message Idea
- Heart of the Message
- Heart of the Messenger
- Historical Context
- Illustration
- Interpretive Insight
- Life Application
- Narrative on Life
- Narrative on the Text
- New Testament Connection
- On the Lighter Side
- Pause for Prayer
- Pause for Reflection
- Quotable Quote
- Significant Scripture
- Word Study

It is important to note that some of the teaching resources listed above will appear in every study (for example, The Heart of the Message, The Heart of the Teacher, and Interpretive Insights). Some of the other resources might appear in one message but not in another. The various components of the OTC messages contained in this teaching guide are defined in the pages that follow. As you review what each of these teaching tools offers, you will begin to get a sense for depth and breadth of what is offered in each of the OTC message resources.

Creative Message Idea

This section of the OTC teaching resource will offer a broad variety of ideas a teacher can use to bring a biblical point home with power. This section will include video pieces developed specifically for OTC messages. These are on the video and DVD included in the OTC kit. This section will also include a number of ideas for using props or visual aids to communicate a relevant biblical truth. Some of the creative message ideas will help the teacher move worshipers to respond or interact during the message. We can't begin to cover all the creative ideas that have been developed to bring the message of the Old Testament alive, but if you take a few moments and skim through this OTC teacher's resource, you will begin to get a sense of the kinds of creative ideas that are available for a teacher or preacher. In an effort to make these ideas user friendly, we have listed everything that is needed to naturally incorporate each creative idea into the message. Each of these ideas has been used effectively at Willow Creek, Corinth Church, or both, but we encourage you to decide which ones will connect in your particular context. Also relevant here is the CD-ROM, which has Power-Point presentations and even a game, "Are You an Old Testament Expert?"

Heart of the Message

This is a brief description of the heartbeat or central theme of *the entire message*. Each message will begin with a short section to help the teacher gain a sense of the core idea or ideas being communicated in each OTC message.

Heart of the Messenger

Teachers and preachers can't communicate with passion and clarity until their hearts have been touched and impacted by the truth of God's Word. This section of the teacher's resource will give some direction for how each teacher can begin to prepare to study and open their heart to what the Holy Spirit wants to say to them. One of the goals of the Old Testament Challenge is to help teachers move forward in their own journey of faith. We believe the process of self-examination, deep learning, and personal growth that will be experienced while leading the OTC can be life-changing! This section will usually include a few questions for personal reflection as the teacher prepares to bring the OTC message.

Historical Context Note

Throughout the teacher's resource you will find helpful notes on the historical context of certain passages. There are a number of texts we will study in the OTC that make much more sense when we have an understanding of the culture and the world of the Old Testament. The Historical Context Notes are provided to help you teach about this kind of background information. These notes are not designed to be highly academic observation but are intended to help the teacher make natural observations about culture and customs that will bring the message of the Old Testament alive.

Illustration

Jesus was a master storyteller. He used word pictures to illustrate much of what he taught. In the teacher's resource we have provided many ideas for illustrating core Old Testament ideas. Sometimes these illustrations can be read just as they are printed in this teacher's guide. At other times, the teacher will be given ideas or direction on developing an illustration out of their own life or ministry. Each teacher must decide whether an illustration fits for their setting. Even if a particular illustration does not fit in your context, it might spark some ideas for an illustration that does.

Interpretive Insight

A huge part of teaching the Bible is doing interpretive work. We have provided solid biblical interpretation that can function as the backbone of each OTC message. This does not mean that the teacher should not do additional study, but it does offer a great starting point. Major texts being used in each message will have a brief, or sometimes extended, section of biblical interpretation provided in the teacher's resource guide.

Life Application

In the book of James we read these words, "Do not merely listen to the word, and so deceive yourselves. Do what it says" (James 1:22). Any study of God's Word that is going to have life-changing power must include application. In each OTC message you will find ideas for life application. Sometimes these ideas are specific. They will give detailed instruction on concrete ways a congregation can respond to God's Word. At other times these applications will be broad, intended to encourage individual reflection upon a specific area of life. In these cases, the specific application will come as the Holy Spirit speaks to the heart of each person and shows where change needs to take place.

Narrative on Life

Occasionally telling a story from everyday life is the best way to bring a biblical truth home to the listeners. In this OTC teacher's guide we have captured some great examples of life narratives that speak powerfully. These can be used as they are found in the teacher's guide, or you can retell them in your own words.

Narrative on the Text

One of the unique gifts John Ortberg has as a preacher is the ability to tell a familiar biblical story in a fresh narrative form. This retelling of the story, including some natural commentary on the text, brings familiar passages alive. These sections of John's sermons have been captured in a form that can be read by the teacher. Or, they can become a source of ideas as you tell the story in a narrative form that fits your style of communication.

New Testament Connection

There are many places where the Old Testament and New Testament intersect. Because most Christ-followers are more familiar with the New Testament, we have tried to make note of natural connection points between these two parts of the Bible. Sometimes the connection is linguistic, at other times it is thematic, and there are also times when a specific Old Testament passage is used in the New Testament. You will find helpful insights on how the Old Testament passage you are studying relates to familiar portions of the New Testament.

On the Lighter Side

Humor can be one of the greatest tools in a sermon. Jesus used irony and humor in his communication, and we can learn to use it as we teach God's Word. In these portions of the teacher's guide you will find two specific kinds of humorous insights. First, we will make note of biblical passages or insights that have a humorous aspect to them. Second, we will give you ideas for stories or jokes that might hit a main theme in the message.

Pause for Prayer

Too often a teacher waits until the end of a message to pray with God's people about what is being taught and learned. Sometimes the best time to pause for prayer is right in the middle of a message. If a point has a strong life application or potential for conviction and transformation, you might want to pause right in the midst of the message and take a few moments for prayer. The Pause for Prayer sections give suggestions for when you might want to do this and how to move naturally into prayer at these times.

Pause for Reflection

We live in a hurried world. Often, we preach and teach with the clock in mind. In our busy world, we need to be reminded that teaching God's Word should always include time for personal reflection. We need to make space for the Holy Spirit to speak to our hearts and touch our lives. The Pause for Reflection portions of the teacher's guide give the teacher ideas for when they might want to pause, right in the middle of the message, and take a moment for silence. These moments can be used to listen, process the lessons that have been learned, and reflect on personal life application goals.

Significant Scripture

Every sermon in the OTC teaching guide is rooted in Scripture. At the beginning of each section of each message is a list of significant Scriptures for that portion of the sermon. Most of the Scriptures listed are included in the message notes, but some are not. Occasionally we will list a related passage because we believe it would be worth studying as you prepare your message. Most of the time there is exposition of the passages listed in the Significant Scripture part of the study, but some of the time these are simply passages we encourage you to use for reflection as you prepare your message.

Quotable Quote

God has spoken powerfully through many of his people through history. We have collected some great quotes from Christians throughout the ages and included them in the studies.

Word Study

Often the background of a word in the Bible helps a passage come alive and make sense. Any time we feel a word needs explanation, we include a short background piece in a word study. Sometimes these word studies give linguistic background; at other times they simply give a broader meaning for a word that might go unnoticed if not highlighted.

God's Greatest Dream

GENESIS 1–2

The Heart of the
MESSAGE

Infants who receive no love, touch, or words of affection can be damaged for life. Some even die. Before they can ever express their need in words, the smallest of babies cry out for the community and tender touch of other human beings. Children and teens long for acceptance and will do almost anything to have a sense that they fit in and belong to some group, club, team, or even a gang—if that's what it takes to satisfy their hunger for community.

This need does not go away as we become adults. There seems to be some deep and unyielding cry of the heart that says, "I don't want to be alone. I need to love and be loved. My heart is crying out for a place where I can be accepted and belong."

From the beginning to the end of our lives, we hunger and long for community. We were not made to be alone, but in loving and life-giving relationship with God and each other. God, who exists in eternal community as Father, Son, and Holy Spirit, invites us into the beauty and wonder of fellowship with him. He also makes it possible for us to connect heart-to-heart with each other. This journey toward authentic community begins in the first verses of Genesis and finds its culmination in the final verses of Revelation. We were made for community, and it is God's plan to bring us into life-giving relationship with him and with each other. The longing of our heart can only be satisfied when we enter God's plan for community.

The Heart of the
MESSENGER

As you prepare to teach this message, take time to do a heart check. Do you live with an increasing awareness that God loves you? Are you overwhelmed with the reality that God loves each person you will encounter today? Are you stunned by the fact that God longs to invite you into deeper and deeper places of community with him and with others?

Ask God to remind you of the simple, yet life-changing truth that you are God's beloved child! Pray for your heart to be expanded with God's love so that as you teach this message, you speak from a place of joy-filled amazement over God's passion and affection for you! As you prepare to lead, ask God to remind you that your need for community is just as deep in those you will be teaching.

**Brief Message
OUTLINE**

1 God created the heavens and the earth and everything in them.

2 God wanted his community to have a wonderful place to live.

3 The climax of creation is men and women in life-giving community with God and each other.

Sermon Introduction

The following chair illustration is a powerful way to help people form a mental picture of the community experienced by the Trinity and also a picture of the human need for community.

INTERPRETIVE INSIGHT | Challenging the Prevailing Worldview

SIGNIFICANT SCRIPTURE

Genesis 1:1

It is fair to say that the first sentence of the Bible is the single most controversial and important sentence that has ever been written. It is hard for us to imagine how the opening words of the Bible challenged and shattered the prevailing worldview.

Reflect on how these words rivaled the conventional wisdom taught in the creation stories of that day. To get a sense for how these words would have hit people in the Old Testament world, you need to use your imagination. Imagine for a moment that you lived in the days the book of Genesis was written and that you have never heard that there is a personal God who created all things and who promises life in heaven. This idea has never entered your thinking.

Rather, since you have grown up in the ancient Near East, you have heard a number of stories about how creation took place. None of these myths involve a loving and personal creator. These myths embrace a belief that the universe is filled with many gods, and all these gods are limited in power and morally fallible. The gods are petty and jealous with one another.

As a result of this worldview, you live in fear and are ruled by superstition. You are in a world with fertility cults that encourage gross sexual immorality. The people around you worship objects like the sun and the moon and even small stone statues. The common belief is that heavenly bodies, like stars, actually have influence over the affairs of human beings.

CREATIVE MESSAGE IDEA | Art That Reflects the Artist

A strong theme in this portion of Scripture and this message is that the created world reflects the heart, character, and attributes of the creator (the artist). You might want to have a number of people from your congregation (2–6 people) bring a piece of art they have created (from children to adults) and have it on display in the entry area of the church or on the teaching platform. Allow people to begin thinking about how art reflects the artist. Use this as a visual tool to lock in on this aspect of the message. These people could bring paintings, drawings, sculptures, or any other visual art form. It might be helpful to have them stand by their piece of art after the service and tell people how their art expresses something unique about themselves as an artist.

You Will Need

- Someone who can contact 2–6 people in your congregation who have an artistic background to see if they can bring a piece of art that expresses something about who they are as a person
- Space in the entry area of your church or on the platform for these pieces of art to be displayed
- Stands for pictures and small tables for sculptures (as many as are needed for those who will be bringing their art work)
- If you have a digital camera and video projection capability, you might want to have someone take pictures of these pieces of art from varied angles and project these on the screen in your sanctuary before the worship service or during your message

You are familiar with practices such as human sacrifice, used in an effort to manipulate the gods and to gain their favor. You are profoundly aware that the view of human beings is low and that the common belief system says that people were created to do the work that the gods didn't want to do. Life is a cycle of conflict between people and the gods, and, in turn, between fellow human beings. Life is not about servanthood; rather, it is a fight for dominance. Immense violence, elimination of the weak, and infanticide are common and acceptable practices.

The central belief is that life is just an endless cycle. Life is, in the words of the scholars, "a wheel of life that rotates around the hub of death." One generation is born, grows old, dies, another one comes along, and so it goes without any meaning or purpose.

Into this horribly destructive belief system these words are spoken: "In the beginning God"—a transcendent, all-powerful, eternal, personal being—"created the heavens and the earth." These words were written, and the world has never been the same.

> *Our culture, civilization, has been so shaped by the Old Testament that it's almost impossible to conceive how these words changed the world.*
>
> THOMAS CAHILL,
> IN THE GIFT
> OF THE JEWS

CREATIVE MESSAGE IDEA | Video of Nature's Beauty

The video provided in Kit 1 of the Old Testament Challenge materials has a visual/music montage that beautifully illustrates the creation story. This video includes music, pictures of creation, and texts from Genesis. The video runs three minutes and twenty seconds and can be used during the worship service, at the start of the message, or in the midst of the message.

You Will Need

- Video projection capability in your worship center
- Someone to run the video during the service

CREATIVE MESSAGE IDEA | A Picture of the Trinity in Community . . . The Three Chairs

Set three chairs on the stage (before the service begins, if possible). Have the chairs facing each other as if three people were sitting in them in intimate conversation. As you begin your message, you might want to invite three people to come and sit in these chairs as a picture of the community. You might also have a fourth chair off to the side, out of community with God. A person in this chair could represent people who are not in intimate relationship with God. These chairs and people can be used to paint a picture of community as you begin your message.

They can be used as you describe the Trinity and how God exists in eternal community. They can be used as you describe the community that God longed to forge with Adam and Eve, his children. As you work on this imagery, you can move in other directions as well. When you look at how community is broken through sin, you can move a chair away to portray separation from God or from community with other people.

This illustration is a simple visual that can be used in this sermon and possibly carried into a future sermon as well. It is a strong way to begin your message. Once you have painted this picture of God's eternal community and his longing to invite us into this wonderful place of fellowship, you can have your volunteers return to their seats (with a big "thank you" for helping out with the message). The chairs can remain where they are so that you can refer back to them as you walk through the message.

You Will Need

- Three chairs facing each other
- One additional chair off to the side

1. God Created the Heavens and the Earth and Everything in Them

It is the first question asked by countless children. As we grow up, we ask it over and over again. It is a good question, a fair question. And it is just one word: "Why?"

We all have a desire to know why things are the way they are. Why am I here? Why is anyone here? In this portion of the message we will address why God created the heavens and the earth. Ultimately, we will answer the question: Why are we here?

....

"Why does something exist rather than nothing?"
It's a great question!

RICHARD SWINBURNE, A GREAT TWENTIETH-CENTURY PHILOSOPHER

SIGNIFICANT SCRIPTURE

Genesis 1:1–3;
James 1:17;
John 1:1, 14; 17:21

INTERPRETIVE INSIGHT | Community from the Beginning

Highlight the presence of the Trinity from the very beginning of creation. Make note of the community that existed even in the creation of the world:

- In verse 1 we see the **Father** creating. In James 1:17 this Creator is called "the Father of the heavenly lights," who sends us every good and perfect gift from above.

- In verse 2 the **Spirit** of God is hovering over the waters. Similar language is used to describe the Spirit of God hovering over Jesus at his baptism.

- In verse 3 God creates by speaking his word. In the beginning of the gospel of John we learn that "the Word" through whom all things are created is none other than Jesus Christ, the **Son of God** (John 1:1, 14).

Out of this community, this Trinitarian joy and delight, God creates. He does not do this because he is bored or because he is lonely. God does not create us so that he will have little servants to do the chores he does not want to do. Rather, out of the magnificent richness of the eternal community experienced by the

NEW TESTAMENT CONNECTION

The Heartbeat of God

John 17:21 captures the heartbeat of the Father and the Son who long to invite us into intimate fellowship. The community of the Trinity is so rich; they long to invite us in to share in the feast. The community God longs to have with his people all the way back in the first chapters of Genesis is still something God desires.

....

CREATIVE MESSAGE IDEA | The Three Chairs (continued)

Use the image of the three chairs and reflect on how God exists in eternal community. He did not create us because he was bored or so that we could do the chores he did not want to do. God's creation of man and woman reflects his very nature, he is a God who exists in eternal community: Father, Son, and Holy Spirit. At this time you might want to add another chair to the circle of three you have on the stage. Let people know that the fellowship of the Father, Son, and Holy Spirit is not closed, but open! God has placed a chair and invites you to come and join this community.

Trinity, God decides to broaden the circle. He longs to invite us to live in his love. This invitation is not for us to become little gods, but it is for us to bask in the glorious fellowship of the Trinity. This is the first open chair in all time. We sit in that chair, and God invites us to enter his circle, to pull up to his table, to join the community of the Father, Son, and Holy Spirit.

God's aim in history is the creation of an inclusive community of loving persons, with himself included as its primary sustainer and most glorious inhabitant.

DALLAS WILLARD

2. God Wanted His Community to Have a Wonderful Place to Live!

We get confused. All of us do, sometimes. We forget that only the Creator is to be worshiped, never the creation. At the time Genesis was written, people worshiped the sun, moon, stars, and even little stone idols. Thankfully, we have moved well beyond that kind of adoration of material things . . . or have we?

Many people have become entangled in new forms of idolatry. Let some of these words float through your mind for a moment: Lexus, Beemer, my portfolio, the summer cottage, or my horoscope, just to name a few. Material things still cry out for our worship, and we need to get a proper perspective on the stuff of this world. We need to remember who made it all, who sustains it all, and who truly deserves our worship and adoration.

You can't buy happiness, but now you can lease it!

MAGAZINE AD FOR A CAR COMPANY

PAUSE FOR PRAYER

You might want to pause right here, in the middle of your sermon, and invite the congregation to pray for the ability to hear and receive God's invitation to enter into the rich and eternal fellowship of the Father, Son, and Holy Spirit.

SIGNIFICANT SCRIPTURE

Isaiah 55:1–2;
Ephesians 2:8–9

NEW TESTAMENT CONNECTION | Celebrating the Creator and His Creation

God created a place where we could enter into community with him and with each other, but we need to live with a deep awareness that the Creator and the creation are infinitely different. Though the creation can reveal things about the nature and character of the Creator, the creation is never to be worshiped. There is a human tendency to get this confused! In the New Testament, the apostle Paul put it this way, "They exchanged the truth of God for a lie, and worshiped and served created things

rather than the Creator—who is forever praised. Amen" (Romans 1:25).

Look at the order of creation and how God made the sun, the moon, and the stars. In the order of creation, the sun and moon were not spoken into existence until the fourth day. This truth spoke volumes to people who worshiped the heavenly bodies. Genesis teaches that the sun and moon are not divine; they are created objects. They were made by the one God who spoke heaven and earth into existence. Not only does the Bible teach

that they have a beginning but also that they will have an end (Revelation 21:23).

A healthy understanding of creation will give us a balanced perspective on material things. We should not be captivated by the stuff of this world; rather, we should worship the One who made it all. Too often in this life we become enamored by material things instead of the Creator. Genesis gives us a true perspective on happiness. We can't buy it, we can't lease it, but God invites us to receive freely what we could never afford.

WORD STUDY

ex nihilo

The following is a phrase taken from the Latin language: *ex nihilo*. Literally it means, "out of nothing." We can create things from the stuff God has already made (wood, metal, clay, etc.). But only God can create *ex nihilo*.

ILLUSTRATION | ## My Story

You might want to tell a story about a time you were in God's creation and learned about his character and beautiful creativity as you looked at all he has made. We need to celebrate the wonder of his creation, but let this celebration turn our eyes beyond the creation to the Creator.

ILLUSTRATION | ## "We Don't Have the Power!"

Seven times we read that God spoke and things came into existence. We are so limited in power, but God can speak and the universe comes into being. In the *Star Trek* series, Captain Kirk often barked out a command, "I need more power!" Often he would hear back from Scottie, "I can't do it, Captain." With all the resources of the Enterprise and all the futuristic instruments they had, there were times when the captain's commands were met with a panicked, "We don't have the power!" When we speak, we see limited results; when God speaks, there is always enough power!

INTERPRETIVE INSIGHT | ## Good Stuff

Another theme in creation we need to notice is that God kept giving a running commentary on his creation. Do you notice how he describes it, over and over again? He says, "It is good." God takes endless delight in his creation.

ILLUSTRATION | ## A Glimpse of God's Love

Many people have a deep love for animals. They have a pet that means so much to them. There is a true story about a guy who chartered a plane and flew his dog across three states just so they could be together. It was just the pilot and the dog on the trip . . . a private plane ride. It might seem strange to some people, but those who really love their pets can understand this story. Now, take the love that guy had for his pet dog and multiply it over and over, and you might get a glimpse of how God feels about his creation.

As a teacher, you can tell this story, or tell a story from your own life about someone you know who did something extraordinary because he or she loved a pet. The key is helping people see that God's love for his creation is so much greater than our love.

Because children have abounding vitality and because they are fierce and free in spirit, they want things repeated and unchanged. They always say, "Do it again," and the grown-up person does it again until he is nearly dead—for grown-up people are not strong enough to exult in monotony. But perhaps God is strong enough to exult in monotony. It is possible that God says every morning, "Do it again," to the sun; and every evening, "Do it again," to the moon.

It may not be automatic necessity that makes all daisies alike; it may be that God makes every daisy separately but never gets tired of making them. It may be that he has the eternal appetite of infancy; for we have sinned and grown old, and our Father is younger than we.

....

God has boundless delight in what he creates.
THE GREAT CHRISTIAN THINKER G. K. CHESTERTON

LIFE APPLICATION | Take Time to Notice

When we celebrate the wonder of creation and this celebration leads us to authentic worship of the Creator, we discover joy. Take time this week to drink in the wonder of God's creation. Go to a forest preserve, the oceanside, the lakeside, or a large park, or just take a long drive. Notice the colors, the birds, the plants, the color of the sky, and whatever else you see. Take time to praise the Creator for the beauty of his handiwork. Tell him, "You know, Lord, you are right! This really is good."

3. The Climax of Creation: Human Beings in Community with God and Each Other

As human beings, we live with the risk of forgetting who we are. We live between two radically different extremes. On the one hand, we can become prideful and believe we deserve a place equal to God. Sadly, this happened early in human history, and it still happens today. On the other end of the continuum is an attitude that degrades human beings and treats them as some coincidental result of a random Big Bang or cosmic accident.

Between these poles lies the truth. We are God's creation. Human beings are the apex, the pinnacle of God's creative work. Yet, we are not God, we are his children. We are valuable because of who made us, and we are significant because of how he made us, in his image! Yet we must never forget that he is the Creator and we are his creation.

INTERPRETIVE INSIGHT | A Healthy Perspective

The first thing we need to notice when we read of the creation of human beings is that we are finite, limited, and fragile. We are not gods. We are made of dust. It is important to note that everything else in creation was spoken into existence. We are told, from the very beginning, something that gives us perspective on life. Genesis 3:19 teaches us that we came from dust and will return to dust.

Big deal,
I'm used to dust.
ERMA BOMBECK

WORD STUDY

Imago Dei

It's time for another brief Latin lesson. Here is a great phrase that has been used for centuries by scholars and theologians: *imago Dei*. It means "the image of God." In Genesis 1:27 we are told that we were created in the image of God. We have the *imago Dei* within us. For example, we have a capacity for community. We don't know all of what it means to be created in the image of God, but our capacity for community is certainly part of it.

INTERPRETIVE INSIGHT | ## More Than Dust

The dominant scientific worldview today says we are simply highly evolved apes without tails. We are just the next step in the evolutionary chain of events. But Genesis tells a different story. We might be made of dust, but we are still the apex of God's creation. The crescendo at the end of this symphony is the creation of men and women, made in the image of God.

INTERPRETIVE INSIGHT | ## God Loves His Creation

Focus on how God relates with his creation and how he continues to build relationship with us:

- God blesses his people and gives abundant life (Genesis 1:28).

- God provides for his people (Genesis 1:29).

- God calls us to meaningful and rich experiences of work (2:15). It is important to note that work is not a result of the Fall, but was a gift given before the Fall. After the Fall work became painful, but before, it was a gift from the hand of the Father. God actually left some things undone and invited us into the joy of being coworkers with him.

ON THE LIGHTER SIDE | ## Woman

Genesis records a charming story about a parade of animals that are brought before Adam to see if any of them might be his type. They are all brought to him, and Adam gives them each a name. It seems Adam is an excellent namer. Naming has to do with studying these creatures and perceiving their natures. Adam is beginning to learn and to work and to add value to the world around him.

Adam looks at each of the animals and says, "Oh, I like it, great job, God. But, to tell you the truth, it's not really my type." So, God creates a woman, and Adam immediately decides she *is* his type. His response is sheer poetry (Genesis 2:23). It really is Hebrew poetry. There's a kind of playfulness to this text. It's hard to translate into English.

In effect, what Adam says is, "She shall be called ʾishsha, for she was taken out of ʾish." These words are somewhat like the words for *man* and *woman* in English. In fact, that's where the old line comes from that Adam sees Eve for the first time and says, "**Whoa, man**—yeah, that's it: **Wo-man**." This play on words in English is similar to the play on words in Hebrew. This kind of wordplay is quite common in Hebrew.

Closing Reflections and Challenges

1. *Invitation to take the Old Testament Challenge.* Give a strong exhortation to commit to the daily study and reflections as well as small group gatherings (if you are a part of these). This might be a good time to remind people about the idea of keeping notes in their Bible and add the four symbols to help them remember what struck them as they studied:

   ? What's up with that?

   ! Pay attention to this command!

   ♥ My heart burned within me. This marks a prompting of the Holy Spirit for life change.

   Δ Lessons about the character of God.

2. *Reissue the challenge to take time in creation and celebrate the Creator and all he has made.* Sound the call to slow down, notice, appreciate, and celebrate God's creation, but also to keep a proper perspective. Praise and worship belong to the Creator, never the creation!

3. *Pray.* Thank God for his amazing invitation into community with him and the people he has created.

Brief Message
OUTLINE

1 Adam and Eve

2 Cain and Abel

3 The days of Noah

4 The tower of Babel

The Heart of the
MESSAGE

God's plan was for community. His desire was for human beings to live in harmonious and loving relationship with him and with each other. God did his part. He made us and gave us a wonderful place to meet with him and enter into rich and life-giving relationship with each other.

Sometimes the best of plans go bad. In Genesis 3–11 we see the downward spiral of sin in four distinct scenes: Adam and Eve, the story of Cain and Abel, the Flood, and the Tower of Babel. As we watch the drama unfold, we see things go from bad to worse. Sin goes deep and spreads wider. We also learn from God's response to the sinful choices made by his children.

In this message we will look into the mirror of God's Word and see ourselves. We will face the reality of our sin and be reminded of the depth of God's grace for his beloved children.

The Heart of the
MESSENGER

This is a message that will invite the Holy Spirit to come and lay every heart bare before the Father. We will look deeply into Scripture and also intently into the mirror to see ourselves as God sees us. The reflection we see is not always attractive!

As a teacher, take time to search your own heart and ask God to show you where there is hidden sin. Take time to read and reflect on Psalm 51 (a prayer of confession David lifted to God after a time of brazen sin and deep brokenness). Ask for God to prepare your heart to teach on a very important but difficult subject.

Sermon Introduction

INTERPRETIVE INSIGHT | The Authorship of the Pentateuch

Scholars believe Moses wrote most of the Pentateuch, but they are pretty confident that he didn't write every word. Because Deuteronomy records the story of the death of Moses, we can be confident he did not write that section. In Numbers 12:3 we read the statement, "Now Moses was a very humble man, more humble than anyone else on the face of the earth." It is difficult to imagine Moses writing, "I was a very humble man, more humble than anyone." The Pentateuch is closely associated with Moses, but there may be some sections that were not written by him.

LIFE APPLICATION | Old Testament Challenge Study

You may want to take a brief moment and make a clarifying comment about the OTC study. There are thirty-two messages in the full OTC program. If you are walking through the full OTC program with your church, here are a couple of points of clarification that will be helpful for those who are participating:

- Walking through the OTC (including the individual reading and small group studies) will give your church members a chance to get strongly grounded in the Old Testament. But, because this is an overview study, there is not enough time to look at every individual chapter of each book in the Old Testament.

- In this study you will spend more time in some books, such as Genesis, than in other books, because Genesis has more foundational material.

- Each message will not correspond with the exact passage that you are reading each week if you are doing the full reading guide. However, the

WORD STUDY

Pentateuch

The first five books of the Bible are called the Pentateuch. The word *Pentateuch* comes from two words: *penta*, which means "five" (as in "pentagon"), and *teuch*, which means "scroll." The word Pentateuch means the five scrolls, because these are the first five books of the Old Testament. The Jews called these books the "Torah," and in the New Testament they are called the "Law." When you read the phrase "the Law and the Prophets," "the Law" refers to these first five books and "the Prophets" refers to the other historical books as well as the prophetic books of the Old Testament. The Pentateuch is essentially the work of Moses. When we look at this portion of the Bible, it is best to see it as one book with five sections.

CREATIVE MESSAGE IDEA | The Three Chairs

Again, use the three chairs to represent the Trinity in perfect community. Set another chair in the middle of them to represent people who are invited into community and intimate relationship with God.

As you look at each of the four scenes that reflect sin and broken community, move the chair in the middle farther and farther from the other three chairs. Let this be a visual reminder,

as you teach, of how sin breaks community and creates greater distance from God.

You Will Need
- Three chairs facing each other
- One additional chair in the middle of the three chairs (it might be helpful to have this chair look different from the other three)

message will line up exactly with the abbreviated reading guide provided in the OTC resources.

- Encourage participants to commit to this series regardless of how much of the Old Testament they decide to read along the way.

1. Adam and Eve

SIGNIFICANT SCRIPTURE

Genesis 2:16–17

Adam and Eve had everything they needed. God had provided a paradise beyond what any one of us could imagine. They had access to all the fruit of the garden . . . with one explicit exception.

What follows is tragic. Rather than celebrating what they had, they fixated on what they did not have. Rather than enjoying what was in-bounds, they wanted what was out-of-bounds. What follows is an account of the temptation they faced, how they fell, and the staggering consequences of this rebellion. Along with the unveiling of the tempting tactics of the devil, we see the relentless love of God for his children. Among the dissonant notes of sin, we hear the strains of grace begin to echo through history.

CREATIVE MESSAGE IDEA | Picture the Downward Spiral of Sin

As you talk about each of the four scenes of how sin impacts our lives and our community with God and each other, add the names of the key people and then draw a downward spiral showing how sin becomes a powerful cycle pushing us further and further from God (see the diagram). This simple visual tool paints a picture in the minds of listeners.

You Will Need:
- A large flip chart or a large, dry-erase marker board
- An easel to hold up the board
- Large, wide-tipped markers

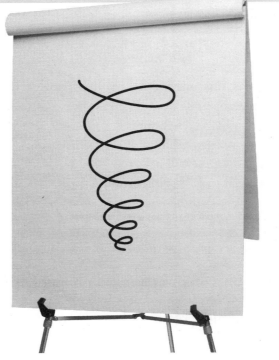

INTERPRETIVE INSIGHT | The Nature of Sin

Sometimes people wonder, "Why did God give this command? If God had not given any commands at all, human beings wouldn't have sinned and everything would have been OK." And people wonder, "Why doesn't God want Adam and Eve to know the difference between good and evil?"

The point of this command is *not* that Adam and Eve will gain moral discernment if they eat from the tree. Moral discernment is a good thing. The idea is that in eating from the tree, they will be declaring, "Now we can decide what is good and evil quite apart from God or anybody else. Now we can be our own God." God is allowing them to choose to be in community with him or to reject community.

SIGNIFICANT SCRIPTURE

Genesis 3:1–6

NARRATIVE ON THE TEXT | The Tactics of the Enemy

The enemy comes into the picture early in human history! He is not called Satan in this story, but the Christian church came to identify the serpent with the evil one. What follows is an absolutely brilliant exposition of how temptation works. This was true at the beginning of time, and it is just as true today!

Tactic of the Enemy 1: He twists the truth.

Satan begins with a lie! He twists the truth and misquotes God. Did God say Adam and Eve could not eat from any tree at all? No. God said they could eat from *every tree except one*. In Genesis 2:9 we're told that there were all sorts of trees that were beautiful to see and the fruit was delicious to eat. Adam and Eve were invited to feast on the fruit of all of them! They could eat from any tree *except one*. But the serpent taunts them by saying that God would not let them eat from any tree at all!

This is a misquote of litigious proportions. What is the serpent up to here? He wants to plant a doubt in the woman's mind. He wants her to doubt the goodness of God. He wants her to think, "I can't trust that God has my best interests at heart. I think if I really obey God fully, I will miss out on something good, so I guess I will have to watch out for myself in this world. I guess I better be prepared to set aside what God says if it's really necessary." The decision to sin always involves these kinds of thoughts. Satan sows seeds of doubt concerning God's goodness, and we have to decide if we are going to entertain those thoughts.

Tactic of the Enemy 2: He wants us to see God as more severe than he is.

In Genesis 3:2 we see a second tactic of the enemy. Eve begins to make God more severe than he really is. The woman corrects the serpent when he speaks deceptive words, but notice one inaccuracy in her account of what God says. Did you catch it? When speaking of the forbidden fruit Eve adds the words, "and you must not touch it." God never said, "You must not touch it." But, in Eve's mind she's making God a little more severe than he really is. She's making him a little unreasonable so that disobeying him becomes a more justifiable act.

Tactic of the Enemy 3: He attacks our vulnerable spots and isolates us.

Another tactic of the enemy is that he will always strike at people's vulnerable points. In Genesis 2:16, when God originally gave the command concerning the forbidden fruit, who was present? It was just the man. So, presumably, where does the woman get her information about what God said? From the man. She gets it secondhand!

Notice something else. As she is engaged in this process of deliberation and dealing with temptation, she does not involve the man. When we play with temptation and do it in isolation, we are in grave danger. The enemy wants us to keep it to ourselves—to keep things hidden in the darkness of our own heart. But, when we don't tell anybody else about our struggle and temptation, we make ourselves infinitely more vulnerable.

That is exactly what Eve did and what we do so often. She didn't talk with God about it. She didn't talk with Adam. She stayed in isolation and dealt with it on her own.

Tactic of the Enemy 4: He wants us to fixate on sin.

Read Genesis 3:6 closely and notice what happens. The implication of this verse is that Eve's mind becomes obsessed with the fruit she is not to eat. She keeps thinking about what she'd miss if she didn't eat it. She keeps looking at it, obsessing over it without God or another person to challenge her thinking. When she does that, the next step becomes inevitable. It's just inevitable that she'll eat it.

Tactic of the Enemy 5: He entices us to invite others into our sin.

When we read the account of sin entering the world, we simply read that Eve gave Adam the fruit, and he ate. Have you ever noticed that sin loves company? So often, when a person enters into sin, they want others to join with them. It is as if we think we will feel better if others are engaged in the same activity.

Does it strike you that the man is a little passive when Eve offers him the fruit? She offers, he takes, he eats! It seems as if Adam did not even think about his actions or the implications. You know what? Sin is often like that. If you ask a child why they do something foolish or destructive, what do they say? "I don't know."

NEW TESTAMENT CONNECTION
The Father of Lies

In John 8:44 we read these words spoken by Jesus about the devil: "He was a murderer from the beginning, not holding to the truth, for there is no truth in him. When he lies, he speaks his native language, for he is a liar and the father of lies." What a powerful reminder that, from the beginning of creation, the tactics and the strategies of the devil have not changed.

If you were to ask Adam, "Adam, why? You had the whole garden with all these wonderful things to eat. God told you not to eat from this one tree. Why did you eat the fruit?" What do you think Adam would say? "I don't know. It seemed like a good idea at the time." Sin really does involve that kind of thoughtlessness.

> *One reason sin flourishes is that it is treated like*
> *a cream puff instead of a rattlesnake.*
>
> BILLY SUNDAY

NARRATIVE ON THE TEXT | The Consequences of Sin

Consequence of Sin 1: The *imago Dei* is marred.

Now immediately we see the consequences. Their eyes were opened. That's what they had been hoping would happen. That's what the serpent promised. But what a nightmare they saw. They looked at each other, and the beauty of the image of God that we talked about last week—the *imago Dei*—had been horribly twisted and marred.

Consequence of Sin 2: Shame.

This man and woman, who had never known shame, looked at each other, and shame filled their hearts. They saw a stranger. They wanted to hide. Something happened to human nature in that moment that we need to be very clear about: Sin entered in. Theologians coined this moment "the Fall."

Consequence of Sin 3: Alienation

The consequences of sin were horrific. Adam and Eve were alienated from themselves, alienated from each other, alienated from their God, alienated from their work, and alienated from creation. Before, they had walked with God in the cool of the garden. Now, when he came to walk with them, they ran away! Alienation had entered the human experience.

SIGNIFICANT SCRIPTURE

Genesis 3:7–24

ON THE LIGHTER SIDE | How Men Communicate

A couple of questions here just for women. How many of you have ever known a man? How many of you have ever known a man to have any kind of communication difficulties? How many of you have known a man who did not always give fully detailed accounts of his conversations and activities? Remember, God gave his instructions to Adam, and Adam had to pass this information on to Eve. Now the enemy is after the one who was not directly present to hear what God said.

WORD STUDY

Depravity

The old theological language for the human condition after sin entered in is *depravity*. This is the birth of shame and guilt. People in our day often speak about believing in the basic goodness of human beings. As Christians, we believe it is very good that God made human beings. We matter to him immensely, and we were made in God's image. It is also true that human beings often do good things. But followers of Christ understand that because of the Fall, human beings are not simply neutral, moral agents who can always choose to do good if we just try hard enough.

Here is the truth: As glass is predisposed to shatter and nitroglycerin is predisposed to explode, we are predisposed to do wrong when the conditions are right. Theologically, that human predisposition is called depravity. In the days of the Reformation, great Christian thinkers even talked about total depravity. The primary idea is that depravity affects all of us—not just our behavior but also our thoughts and our feelings. God's Word is clear that we cannot fix this problem on our own. We need God's help.

Consequence of Sin 4: Fear

When God asks Adam where he is, Adam makes an amazing statement. He tells God that he was afraid and was hiding. Wow! This is the first mention of fear in the Bible. Sin creates fear in our hearts and drives us away from the very one, the only one, who can remove the pain and consequences of our sin.

Consequence of Sin 5: Blame

God confronts Adam and asks him if he has broken God's commandment and eaten fruit from the tree that was clearly off-limits. When facing this direct and incriminating question, Adam carefully reflects on the importance of taking personal responsibility for his actions. He summons up all of his courage and says, "The woman *you* put with me—she wasn't my idea. She is at fault!" Adam is not giving any more of that "bone of my bone" stuff. Not anymore. You can almost hear Adam saying, "When it was just me and the animals, everything was OK. But that woman, she sure has gotten us into a lot of trouble!" At this moment, blaming enters human history. Do you think they'll be the last married couple to blame each other?

Consequence of Sin 6: Pain

One of the greatest lies the enemy has ever told is when he said, "You will not surely die." The moment Adam and Eve disobeyed God and ate the fruit, death began to set in all around them. Certainly physical death began, but the consequences of sin were deeper and wider. The *imago Dei* ("image of God") was marred, shame filled their hearts, relational death began, alienation took hold, fear consumed them, and the blame game started. On top of all of this, Adam and Eve faced a new reality—pain!

The woman is told she will face pain (labor) in her delivery of children. The man is told he will experience pain (labor) in his work. In the Hebrew, the language gives the sense that the curse is similar for both the man and the woman—pain has entered into the human experience. They will also face the relational pain that grows out of all the consequences already listed.

The battle and strife between men and women goes on to this day as a result of the Fall. The wonderful oneness we saw in Genesis 1 and 2 has been shattered. Spiritual death began on that day, and physical death as well.

> *Depravity is a spiritual condition that involves our readiness to harm others or at least let harm come to them if that will help us reach our goals of security, ego-gratification, or the satisfaction of our deep desires. Depravity is this: We would like to do what's right, but we're prepared to do what's wrong if we feel it's necessary for our survival or well-being.*
>
> PARAPHRASE OF DALLAS WILLARD IN *THE SPIRIT OF THE DISCIPLINES*

ILLUSTRATION | ## Will You Share? No

There are all kinds of examples of depravity. We just need to look at our lives and the lives of those around us, and we can find signs of this spiritual reality everywhere. Think for a moment about a two-year-old child. What are the odds that if you make a two-year-old share a toy that he's been hogging, he'll say, "I'm so glad it brings you joy. Would you like to use my blankey as well?" Think about it. Do you need to teach a child to be selfish? No! This comes quite naturally. What we have to teach is generosity and selflessness! This is just one sign of depravity.

INTERPRETIVE INSIGHT | ## Why God Asks Questions

Through the whole Bible, God often asks questions. In Genesis 3:9 we hear God say to Adam, "Where are you?" It is important for us to note that God is not asking because he can't find Adam. God knows exactly where Adam is (physically and spiritually). What God is doing is giving Adam a chance to show himself and confess. This question is a great sign of God's amazing grace. Each time you hear God ask a question in the Bible, stop and reflect. If God already knows the answer, why is he asking the question?

INTERPRETIVE INSIGHT | ## Who's in Charge Here?

Many people believe that a husband's ruling over his wife was part of God's original plan. To some people, this might even seem like a good idea. But as we study the Bible, it becomes clear that this was one of the results of the Fall. This is part of the curse. Here is the good news: God has come to set us free from the power of sin and the curse. God's plan is for husbands and wives to walk together in harmony and find the place of oneness that existed before the Fall.

WORD STUDY

Walking

In the Old Testament, walking with God is a picture of intimate communion. Sin destroyed Adam and Eve's desire for this intimacy, but God still wanted it. They were ready to run away, but God wanted to walk with them. This word "walking," when used in the context of walking with God, is powerful. It is a sign that God longs for close friendship with the people he has created. Here is an encouraging reminder: God still wants to walk with us today!

INTERPRETIVE INSIGHT | Grace Notes

As we study Genesis 3, it is not all bad news. Tucked right in this section about sin, depravity, and the Fall are two hope-filled notes of grace. First, God tells the serpent (verse 15) that there will be enmity between him and the woman (including her offspring). We also learn that the serpent will strike at his heel, but the woman's offspring will crush the serpent's head. This passage is talking about Jesus Christ. Right after sin enters in, God is already giving a promise of salvation. Jesus will crush the enemy and destroy the power of sin. This is the first prophetic mention of the coming of the Messiah in all of Scripture. It comes in response to the first sin.

Another grace note in this passage is seen when God made garments of skin for Adam and Eve. At this point Adam and Eve were running around in stitched fig leaves, and they looked severely fashion-challenged. So God became a tailor, and he clothed them so they could come into his presence without being overwhelmed by shame. What a picture of God's grace and love!

If we look closely, we see that there is even more going on here. Because these coverings were made of skin, we know a sacrifice had been made. For the first time in history, innocent blood is shed so that human shame might be covered and human fellowship with God be restored. God is setting the stage for the Passover, and later for the death of Jesus as the sacrifice for our sins. What a powerful reminder of God's grace in these opening pages of the Bible.

ON THE LIGHTER SIDE | What's Happening to Eve?

Try to imagine what it must have been like when Eve became pregnant. There was no precedent. This was all new territory. One day, something happens to Eve. She feels a little nauseous. She starts to get a little moody. She has strange cravings. This has never happened before. There are no books for Eve to read to explain what is happening to her.

One day Adam makes an innocent little observation. "Hey, Eve, you're putting on a little weight there. Your old garments don't fit so well. We'll have to get you a new skin—from a much larger animal this time—like a buffalo or something."

About nine months later a new life enters the world. Here we see again how important names are to the story of the Old Testament. Eve gives this baby the name "Cain." Then she says, "With the help of the Lord I have brought forth a man."

This is typical of women to this day. When they give birth, they mention God a lot and don't express much appreciation to their husbands.

2. Cain and Abel

After the Fall Adam and Eve must have wondered: Would God still continue his plan to fill the earth with human beings, now that they had sinned? Or would it be only the two of them until death? Was this the end of the story, or would there be another chapter? The story of Cain and Abel begins with hope, but soon sin enters in again.

As you look at the story of Adam and Eve and then the story of Cain, you will notice some profound differences in how sin enters in and impacts human community. Eve had to be persuaded by an external tempter to do wrong; Cain had no one tempting him—just his own sinful heart. Adam and Eve's sin was to eat fruit; Cain committed the murder of his brother. Adam and Eve accept their judgment from God without protest; Cain complained that God was being too harsh. This time, the stain of sin went deeper into the fabric of God's beautiful tapestry of community.

SIGNIFICANT SCRIPTURE

Genesis 4

INTERPRETIVE INSIGHT | The Law of Firstfruits

Every time Adam and Eve look at Cain, they are reminded of God's grace. God did not let their sin kill his dream. Then Abel comes along—another gift from God. He is another reminder that God still has plans for the human race.

As time passes, both Cain and Abel bring sacrifices to God. Cain is a farmer, so he brings produce. Abel is a rancher, so he brings an animal sacrifice. God looks with favor on Abel's sacrifice but not on Cain's. People wonder why. Some think that Abel's sacrifice was accepted because it was a blood sacrifice, but I don't think that is what is going on here. I think the best explanation for this lies in a close look at the language. Abel's offering came from the *firstborn* in his flock.

There is a principle in Scripture that the firstborn belongs to God. There's something called the "law of the firstfruits." The idea is that when the very first returns appear—the firstfruits of the tree, the first calf to be born, the first of the harvest brought in—this is to be given to God as an act of trust that he will continue to provide. Abel was living by this principle. He brought what came first, that which was a sacrifice to give. Abel's offering cost him something and required trust!

By contrast, Cain's offering appears to be quite casual. God sees this. He doesn't say he rejects Cain, nor does he even say he is angry. He just sees when a heart is devoted to him and when a heart is going through the motions. At this point, Cain could have done a heart check and recognized his own apathy. This could have been a wake-up call. Instead, he broods, resents, and begins to envy his brother.

LIFE APPLICATION | The Firstfruits

In a world of scarcity we declare that we won't wait until it's easy to give back to God. We will give the firstfruits as an act of trust that God is going to provide for our future. That's what Abel did. That's what Cain refused to do. That's what we're called to do every time the offering plate gets passed. The law of the firstfruits is still in effect today. The question is: Are we living with a faith that produces deep trust that God will provide?

You might want to challenge people to look closely at their giving patterns and ask themselves if they are giving God from their firstfruits or simply tossing God the leftovers.

LIFE APPLICATION | Beware of Envy

Notice that Cain doesn't envy Abel's wealth or success. What does he envy? Cain envies his brother's *spiritual status*. Envy can strike anywhere and anyone! Even spiritual people are susceptible. You might even say that spiritual people are especially susceptible to envy! This should be a clear warning for teachers, small-group leaders, pastors, church-board members, and anyone who serves God. Read Genesis 4:6–7 slowly and carefully: "Why are you angry? Why is your face downcast? If you do what is right, will you not be accepted? But if you do not do what is right, sin is crouching at your door; it desires to have you, but you must master it." These words of warning need to be heard with great clarity today!

INTERPRETIVE INSIGHT | An Invitation to the Light

Notice that God asks another question in Genesis 4:9. What's happening here? Is God unaware of what has happened? Is God looking for Cain because he can't find him? No!

God is graciously playing counselor. He is inviting Cain to come into the light, to acknowledge the condition of his heart, to make this right. God is inviting Cain to come clean and confess. There is this warning, "Sin is crouching at your door," like a beast in you; it will consume you if you let it.

What do we learn as we read on? Cain prefers the darkness. Look at verse 8 and notice how the writer keeps repeating the word "brother" to underscore the tragedy. God is calling Cain to a place of repentance over the murder of his brother. Cain is fighting to stay in the darkness. He says, "Am I my brother's keeper?" Notice that Cain is distorting God's words. "What? Do you expect me to watch him every second?" This is Cain's way of pushing aside God's intent: "Cain, come clean." So God has to pronounce judgment yet again.

HISTORICAL CONTEXT

Good Fat

Notice that Abel gives "fat portions from some of the firstborn of his flock." In our day, fat has negative connotations. We figure *Lean Cuisine* is much more spiritual. But in their day, the battle was against starvation. The fat was the most desirable part, the most life-giving part. Abel chose to give what cost him most and required the greatest trust.

INTERPRETIVE INSIGHT | A Severe Mercy

God tells Cain that he will be driven from community and become a restless wanderer. God knows that if Cain stays in community, he will bring more destruction to God's creation. Cain has broken community and lost sight of God's great dream. But God again offers a kind of severe mercy. Cain complains that someone will kill him in revenge, so God places a mark on him. This is the mark of Cain. It's a reminder of Cain's sin, but it's also a mark of divine protection, a pronouncement that his life is not to be taken. Isn't it amazing to see how quickly God follows judgment with grace?

3. The Days of Noah

There are a few exceptions, but as we move through Genesis the world seems to go from bad to worse. Just read Genesis 6:5: "The LORD saw how great [human] wickedness on the earth had become, and that every inclination of the thoughts of his heart was only evil all the time." And Genesis 6:11–12: "Now the earth was corrupt in God's sight and was full of violence. God saw how corrupt the earth had become, for all the people on earth had corrupted their ways." When we read the story of Cain, we saw how sin went deeper. As we study the days of Noah, we see how sin goes wider.

SIGNIFICANT SCRIPTURE

Genesis 6

INTERPRETIVE INSIGHT | "And God Saw"

When we read, "And God saw" in Genesis 6:12, it's the first time this phrase has been used since Genesis 1. Back in Genesis 1 the phrase is followed, over and over again, by, "It was good." Now there is a dramatic shift. The phrase appears again, but this time it is followed by the words, "It was ruined!" There is a clear sense that this contrast shows that God's good plan has been corrupted.

INTERPRETIVE INSIGHT | One Bright Spot

There's one bright spot left on the earth. His name is Noah! It is as if God says, "The only way this dream can be kept alive is to start over again. The level of corruption is so high there is no other way." So we learn that God is going to send a flood. He gives Noah some instructions. Noah goes to the local hardware store, places a really big order, and the rain begins to fall forty days and forty nights (Genesis 7). Noah obeys God, and God begins his dream again. God says to Noah, in a sense, "I will establish my covenant with you." And God gives Noah a sign to seal this covenant agreement: the rainbow.

4. The Tower of Babel

The story of Babel and the sin of the people is almost a satire on the folly of human arrogance. It is not a commentary on architecture but on the heart of human beings. The people decide to build a tower up to God. This is the same old story of human sin. "We can become like God. We can build something that reaches to the heavens—the place where God lives. Our ultimate devotion will be to ourselves and to the accumulation of power, wealth, and fame." The story of Babel is a reminder of the cycle of sin that human community can fall into. We need to remember that God has called them to multiply and fill up the earth. Instead, they decide to defy God's command and stay centrally located—all in one place. This is just another example of human defiance!

INTERPRETIVE INSIGHT | Looking Down

Now in Genesis 11:5, where does the Lord come to see the Tower of Babel? What direction does he move? Down. Again, this is irony. Where were they going to build their tower? Up to the heavens. God sits in the heavens and looks down and says, "Look at that little tiny bump down there. I guess I'll have to go down to get a closer look."

INTERPRETIVE INSIGHT | Moving East

Be sure to take notice of where Babel was located. Also take note of which direction the people moved when they left Eden. It was eastward. Ever since the Fall there has been a movement east—farther and farther from paradise.

For the Israelites, the Mediterranean Sea was on their west. The east was the place of danger, hostility, enemies, and the loss of community. They did not want to move east anymore. East of Eden becomes this picture of the loss of God's precious dream.

SIGNIFICANT SCRIPTURE

Genesis 11:1–9

NEW TESTAMENT CONNECTION

"If" We Confess

Since the Garden of Eden, the need for human beings to confess their sin has always been profound. Fortunately, we serve a God who invites us to come to him with broken hearts and to seek his grace. In 1 John 2:9 we read, "If we confess our sins, he is faithful and just and will forgive us our sins and purify us from all unrighteousness."

ON THE LIGHTER SIDE | An Investment in Eight-Track Tapes

When we look at Genesis 11:3, we see that the writer is ridiculing human arrogance. He points out that the people of Babel are building with bricks instead of stones! Historically we know that in Babylon, home of Babel, they actually did build with bricks. In Israel they used stone.

Which lasts longer? Stone or brick?

The answer is stone . . . by many times over.

The writer is saying, with some irony and humor, "They think they're building like gods, and they don't even know enough to build with stone rather than bricks. They don't even know the latest technology."

In our day, it would be a bit like saying, "I have a great idea, I am going to invest all of my money in eight-track tapes! I think they are going to make a real comeback. If that goes well, I'll sink my profits into record albums."

ILLUSTRATION | The Downward Spiral of Sin

Either use Power Point or make a drawing of how people kept spiraling deeper and deeper into sin and farther from God. Show how this movement can be symbolized as a movement east and away from God's plan for paradise in human community.

LIFE APPLICATION | Facing Sin Head-On

In Genesis 6 we learn that God's heart is filled with pain because of human sin. This is not trivial. Even though sin has been trivialized in our society, it still matters to God. Just think about it. Outside the church, the only place where you see the word "sin" is on dessert menus in restaurants. It is time for followers of Christ to take a personal inventory and be sure they are taking sin seriously.

The enemy, who was in the garden, whispers to you and to me just as he did to the people back in Genesis. Sin still crouches at the door of the human heart. We might be tempted to gloss over it, deny it, blame it on someone else, or compare ourselves to somebody we think is worse, but we need to face sin head-on.

> *To yield and give in to our sinful desires is the lowest form of slavery. To rule over such desires is the only true freedom.*
>
> JUSTIN MARTYR (SECOND CENTURY)

PAUSE FOR REFLECTION

A Time to Confess

Take time as a leader and invite people to come before God with humility, to come out of hiding, to do what Cain would not do. Invite people to take a few moments to reflect on any temptation or sin they need to confess to God. Ask them to close their eyes. Invite the Holy Spirit to search their hearts. Call God's people to a place of humble repentance.

ON THE LIGHTER SIDE | No Hablo Inglés

Something happens at Babel that is rather funny if you think about it. Up to this point, all people have spoken the same language. Now, all of a sudden, one guy says to the other, "Can I borrow a hammer?" And the guy next to him says, "No hablo Inglés." Up to this point, they used to just speak Swedish (or the language of your choice for your context)—the language of heaven. Now their languages are confused, and they are scattered across the earth.

It's Time to DTR (Define the Relationship)

GENESIS 12–22

Brief Message
OUTLINE
Four defining moments
in the life of Abraham:

1 The call to leave

2 The cutting of a
  covenant

3 The call to hope

4 A call to deeper faith

The Heart of the
MESSAGE

We have all experienced what it is like to hit the pivotal moment in life when we need to do a DTR: "Define The Relationship!"

A couple has been dating for a number of months, things are going well, and everyone seems happy with how things are proceeding. Then things begin to get a little more serious. Both parties involved are wondering, "Is this the real deal?" One, the other, or both sense the need to sit down and ask the big questions, "What are we doing here? Where are we going? What comes next in this relationship? Is this the one for me?" This is a DTR! It is one of those tipping points where things can go one way or the other. A DTR is when we have to ask ourselves, "Am I going to take the next step forward in this relationship and take things to the next level?"

Abraham discovered that DTR moments happen with God all through life if we are paying attention and are ready to respond. Over and over God invited Abraham to a new place of intimacy, a new level of commitment, and a deeper place of community. In each case, Abraham moved out of the DTR moment into a new place of faith. In the same way, God invites us to keep taking steps of faith as we walk with him. He wants us to tune in and recognize when we have DTR moments so that we can respond and go to deeper places of faith and love.

The Heart of the
MESSENGER

The God of Abraham is the same God we worship today! He still speaks to, prompts, and leads his children. He still wants to have profound moments when he can do a DTR with each one of us. As you prepare your heart to teach this message, invite God to do a DTR. Ask the Holy Spirit to search you and open your eyes to see areas in which you hunger for deeper places of faith and love.

Take time to read Psalm 139:23–24 and Psalm 103:1–5. Then wait in silence and invite the Spirit to challenge, convict, encourage, bless, or do whatever he wants to do in your heart. As you prepare to teach about DTR moments in the spiritual life of a follower of Christ, be sure you give God space to have a DTR moment with you!

Sermon Introduction

CREATIVE MESSAGE IDEA | Bendable People

At the very beginning of the message, invite a couple from the congregation to volunteer to help you present a brief visual picture of some DTR moments in human relationships. You might want to ask a couple before the service and be sure you get a married couple who really loves each other and who have some warmth and energy. Use three or more scenarios and comment briefly after each one that these are defining moments in life.

With each scenario, tell the couple where to stand, how to posture themselves, and how to look at each other. Then, read a statement (provided below) and ask for the appropriate person of the couple to respond both physically and in their facial expressions.

Scenario 1: He stands facing the congregation with his hand to the side of his head as if he is holding a phone receiver. She stands off to the side, also holding a receiver to her ear. Then you read the following statement and ask *him* to respond.

They have gone out on a first date and he is crazy about her. He is waiting to hear what she thinks about him. She calls and says these words to him, "I think you have a really nice personality, but I just don't feel any spark. I'm sorry . . . goodbye."

Scenario 2: She stands facing the congregation with her hands in front of her as if she is holding and reading a letter. He stands off to the side with one palm turned up and the other hand set as if he is writing a letter to her on paper held in his hand. Then you read the following words and ask *her* to respond.

They have been dating for a time and she has written him her first love note. She has bared her soul and heart. She has taken a risk and signed the letter, "With all my love." She is now reading his letter of response. It is a kind letter, it is a polite letter, it is a cordial letter, and it is signed, "Your brother in Christ."

Scenario 3: They stand facing each other and holding hands, looking eye to eye. You read the following words and ask *him* to respond.

CREATIVE MESSAGE IDEA | Deb Poling Video Testimony

The video provided in Kit 1 of the Old Testament Challenge materials has a testimony that can be used well in connection with this sermon or worship service. You can use this here in week 3 (or even in week 2 if you feel it fits better there). The goal of the Deb Poling testimony is to inspire people to begin the Old Testament Challenge reading early on in the process.

You Will Need
- Video projection capability in your worship center
- Someone to run the video during the service

They have been dating for six months. He thinks she is the one! They are out on a date. She looks into his eyes, swallows hard, and says, "I really like you. You are a very special person! But . . . I think it would be best for both of us if we were just . . . (pause here) friends!"

Scenario 4: Again they stand facing each other, looking eye to eye. They have been dating for two years, they are very serious, and both feel they are in love. Tell them that this time *both of them* are invited to respond.

He says to her, "It's been two years since we started dating, I am in love with you, you are the one for me, my heart is bursting, my passion is great, I think we are finally ready for our first kiss!"

Then shout . . . "Action!"

(This can be a fun moment, but be sure you know the couple won't be embarrassed.)

Scenario 5: He kneels on one knee and looks up into her eyes. She holds his hands and looks down longingly. Be sure to encourage sincere, longing looks! Read the following words and ask *her* to respond.

He looks into her eyes, thinking of the years of their friendship and growing love. He clears his throat, swallows, and chokes out the words, "Will you marry me?"

Scenario 6: They are standing at the door of their home holding hands as the last guest leaves their fiftieth wedding anniversary party. With their free hands they both wave goodbye. As they stand side-by-side, holding hands, you read the following words and invite both of them to respond.

She leans over to him and whispers in his ear, "I love you more today than I did fifty years ago! How 'bout another fifty?"

INTERPRETIVE INSIGHT God's Plan

As we continue in this study of Genesis we might wonder, will God run out of patience? Is his dream of community broken beyond repair? When we get to

---

HISTORICAL CONTEXT Covenant

A covenant is "a means to establish a binding relationship where none existed before, based on faithfulness to a solemn vow." Faithfulness is the core virtue of covenant behavior. There were different kinds of covenants back in ancient days. Sometimes they were *unilateral*—a covenant between unequal partners. An example of a unilateral covenant would be between a king and his subjects. There were also *bilateral* covenants, which were established between equals. An example of this would be a covenant between friends.

In the Old Testament we find references to "covenant" 285 times. As you read the Old Testament, you can't help but note that God is the God of the covenant; he is characterized by covenantal love. Sometimes this is referred to as "steadfast love." The covenant term "steadfast love" reminds us that God is the One who makes promises out of the depth of his love. He is also the One who always keeps his promises.

Genesis 12, we discover that God still has plans for his children. God will begin again, but this time with a new strategy. He'll work with one man. His name is Abram. God will rename him Abraham, and he will be the father of many nations. God will call Abraham to a series of DTRs as we watch on. In this section of Scripture, Abraham discovers the ultimate DTR: a covenant.

Through Abraham something remarkable is happening. God, who created the heavens and the earth, is entering into a relationship with an ordinary human being. God is promising himself to fallen people. As we look at Abraham's life we discover four dramatic encounters he had with God that kept clarifying their relationship.

DTR 1: The Call to Leave

God has a single command for Abraham: Leave! Leave your country, your people, your tribe, and your father's household—everything safe and familiar. Implied in this is also the call to leave his old gods. Abraham did not know this God who was calling him to this radical step of faith. In Joshua 24:2, Joshua is talking to the Israelites: "Long ago your forefathers, including Terah the father of Abraham and Nahor, lived beyond the River and worshiped other gods." Yet here is Abraham, faced with an epic DTR moment. Will he stay, or will he leave and follow this God who is calling him?

There's an Old Testament principle here. It might be called the "Principle of Separation." God says, "Be separate from other gods—old values, old priorities—and be separate for the one true God." This principle was in effect for Abraham, and it is still in effect for us today.

WORD STUDY

Abram and Abraham

As we have been learning, names were very important in the Old Testament. Most names had significant meaning. This was certainly true for Abraham. When we first meet him, we discover his name is Abram, which means "exalted father." Later, God gives him the name Abraham; this means "father of many nations." As you study Genesis, you will discover the importance of this name change.

SIGNIFICANT SCRIPTURE

Genesis 11:31–12:4

ON THE LIGHTER SIDE | Traveling Without a Map

God tells Abraham, "Leave your country, your people and your father's household and go!" Go where? "Go to the land I will show you." Let's be honest, these instructions are a little vague! There is not much here for Abraham to tell Sarah. And, as many of us know, wives like to have details about these sorts of things.

Imagine the conversation they must have had. And remember, these are real people. Just think of what this interaction would have sounded like: "Sarah, pack up all our belongings. We're moving away from everyone and everything familiar to us."

"Where are we going?"

"I don't know exactly. I'll know it when I see it."

You have to believe that Sarah would have asked what any wife would ask: "How will we know if we get lost? Whom will we ask for directions?"

Abraham replies, "We won't get lost. God will tell me when we get there."

"God who?" Remember, Sarah didn't know this God.

"I didn't catch his last name."

This would be the only trip in human history when a wife would say, "Where in the world are we?" and her husband would say, "God only knows," and he'd be speaking literal truth!

Bless

God gave Abraham a promise. It involved something bigger than he could have imagined. The essence of the promise was one word.

As we read through Scripture, it is always important to look for words that are repeated numerous times in a passage. When this happens, they often carry a lot of weight. Notice in this passage what word is repeated over and over. (You might want to pause as people look at their Bibles to discover this word for themselves.)

The word is simple, yet powerful: *bless.*

The word "bless" or "blessing" or "blessed" is repeated five times in this passage. God says, "I will make you into a great nation." We already know that Abraham and Sarah were childless. Yet God says, "I will make your name great."

Our Heavenly Father never takes anything from his children unless he means to give them something better.
GEORGE MUELLER

INTERPRETIVE INSIGHT | Abraham's Home

We have to understand the choice that Abraham is facing. Abraham is not some uncouth nomad with nothing to lose. He is a prosperous merchant. In verse 5 we read that he has accumulated many possessions, enough to have a whole retinue of servants and slaves. He lives in an urban setting in civilized Mesopotamia.

Haran, where Abraham's family came from, was located far in the northwest part of Mesopotamia. It is listed in Ezekiel 27:23 as one of the great commercial centers of the ancient world. It's on the Euphrates River. In that metropolitan center Abraham is known, respected, and secure. It is a place of safety and familiarity.

Yet Abraham is told to leave for a wilderness where he has no lands, no networks, no connections, and no prospects. This move, humanly speaking, is financial, vocational, and maybe literal suicide. What kind of a person would follow a call like that?

INTERPRETIVE INSIGHT | Abraham Went

The whole story of Abraham (in a sense, the whole story of the Old Testament) hinges on a single phrase in Genesis 12:4. In Hebrew it's two words—*wayyelek ʾabram.* It means "Abraham went" or "Abraham left." As we read these two words, it is important to remember that Abraham was seventy-five years old. Just think about it. Abraham was seventy-five years old and he chose to bet everything on God. He went. He left. He took a step of faith!

The history of all the great characters of the Bible is summed up in this one sentence: They acquainted themselves with God, and acquiesced to His will in all things.
RICHARD CECIL

LIFE APPLICATION | What Can I Leave Behind?

Is God asking you to leave anything? Is he calling you to walk away from some idol, any sin, or some fear? Is God calling you to go someplace, to take a step of faith, to risk for him, or to start serving in some new area of ministry? Do you ever trust God as Abraham did? This is not to say that Abraham was a pillar of spiritual perfection. He had his flaws—and so do we—but he stepped out in faith, and God calls us to do the same.

DTR 2: The Cutting of a Covenant

Some things in life make sense and some things just seem to baffle us! God's desire to enter a covenant with Abraham (and with us) is one of those things that seems almost beyond comprehension. He has everything and we have so little (and what we have has been given by him!). Yet, God initiates an agreement with Abraham, and through him with us. This agreement or covenant reveals the depth of love God has for us as his children. When we enter a covenant relationship with the living God, we face the most significant DTR moment of our lives.

INTERPRETIVE INSIGHT | God's Covenant with Abraham

As noted above, the ancient world saw bilateral covenants (between two equal partners) and unilateral covenants (between a stronger and a weaker partner). The covenant between God and Abraham was clearly unilateral.

Generally speaking, in unilateral covenants the stronger partner always had an agenda. The covenant was based on the idea that there was something the stronger partner could gain from the weaker partner. In Abraham's day, the stronger partner in a covenant was usually after water rights, land to graze his herds on, or something else that would benefit the stronger party in the agreement. Here is the key question we need to ask: "What is God going to get out of this deal? He knows the human race. He knows he will be facing heartache, ingratitude, folly, and sin. So what does he get out of this covenant?"

He gets someone to bless! He gets someone on whom to pour out all of the affection and warmth and mercy and love of his heart, even though it's going to break his heart. This is why the Old Testament writers are staggered by the fact that the God who created the heavens and the earth would choose to enter into a covenant with fallen human beings.

INTERPRETIVE INSIGHT | God's Chosen People

It is important for us to understand what the Old Testament means when it calls Abraham, or Israel, the "chosen people." Some take this to mean that these people are chosen as God's favorites or that they have an inside track to getting into heaven. Because of this perspective, others find this arrangement unfair or arbitrary on God's part.

But when the Bible talks of God's chosen people, it means that Abraham and his descendents were chosen by God to be a kind of model community. This is not for their sake alone, but for the sake of the whole world. The privilege of this calling is the call to serve.

PAUSE FOR REFLECTION
A Step of Faith
Take time to pray and reflect on what you might leave behind so you can follow God with a deeper level of commitment. Allow a few moments of silence during the message and challenge people to do business with God then and there.

SIGNIFICANT SCRIPTURE
Genesis 14:8–24; 15:9–19; 17:1–14

You could put it like this: God so loved the world that he made a covenant with Abraham that all the peoples of the world should be blessed through him. Look at what Paul writes to the Galatians in Galatians 3:8: "The Scripture announced the gospel [or good news] in advance to Abraham when it said: 'All nations will be blessed through you.'"

INTERPRETIVE INSIGHT | The Sign of the Covenant

The sign of Abraham's covenant was circumcision. One of the aspects of circumcision, obviously, is that it's a very physical reminder of the covenant. The physical sign was for males only. It was not done to females, but it did include everybody in a corporate sense. This sign of the covenant was also available to people who were not Hebrews. They too could be a part of the circumcised covenant people. One important element to note is that when God called Abraham to institute circumcision, he obeyed *that very day*.

LIFE APPLICATION | The Beginning of Evangelism

Evangelism in the Bible doesn't really start with the Great Commission. Evangelism starts in Genesis 12:3. God wants to bless the whole earth. He wants to do it through Abraham and this model community, but his desire is not to bless Israel for Israel's sake. It's to bless his people, and then, through his people, to bless everybody on earth. That's God's heart from the very beginning. God doesn't want to leave anybody out.

This should be a clear reminder to each person who knows what it is to be called a child of God and one of his chosen people. We are blessed to be a blessing, and we are called to invite others into his family. Invite each person present in your audience to identify one person who is outside of the family. Challenge them to identify one practical way God might use them to be a blessing to this person in the coming week.

ON THE LIGHTER SIDE | Noah Got a Rainbow

Imagine that you are Abraham. God comes to you and says, "There's going to be a sign for our covenant." (Covenants often had signs that functioned as a constant reminder of the agreement that had been established.) Then God continues, "This is the sign for our covenant: I want you to be *circumcised*."

Now, imagine you, as Abraham, have just received the news. Don't you feel a bit like saying, "Hey! Noah got a rainbow. It doesn't seem quite fair. Couldn't we make our sign something a little more gentle, like a cloud, a secret handshake, a decoder ring, or something like that?"

NARRATIVE ON THE TEXT | Abraham's Ups and Downs

The very first words of Abraham ever recorded in Scripture are, "As he was about to enter Egypt, he said to his wife Sarai, 'I know what a beautiful woman you are. When the Egyptians see you, they will say, "This is his wife." Then they will kill me but let you live. Say you are my sister, so that I will be treated well for your sake and my life will be spared because of you.'"

This is not a great moment in the history of husbanding. Sarah ends up getting stuck in Pharaoh's harem, and God has to intervene. Pharaoh ends up giving Abraham a lesson on integrity, which apparently doesn't strike a real deep cord, because in Genesis 20 Abraham uses the same lie on another king named Abimelech. Let's be honest: Abraham was not a pillar of spiritual perfection.

However, in chapters 13 and 14 he gets some things right, especially as they relate to possessions. In chapter 13 there's a conflict between Abraham's staff and the employees of his nephew Lot over grazing rights. Abraham deliberately gives Lot first choice of whatever land he wants. As the older uncle, Abraham could have insisted on getting his own way, but he is both humble and generous. Because he does this, Abraham experiences the blessing of his generous God.

In chapter 14, Lot is captured in a battle that involves some local chieftains. A coalition from the East comes and defeats a local coalition. Abraham has 318 trained soldiers on his staff (a clear sign of his prominence), and he takes them as he rescues his nephew Lot.

The two kings Abraham interacts with in chapter 14 represent two different ways of dealing with possessions. One of them, the king of Sodom, offers to allow Abraham to keep the spoils of war. He says, "You can keep your stuff," but with the implicit condition that Abraham will now owe allegiance to him. The message of this king is that powerful men are allowed to grab and keep whatever they can. He invites Abraham to be part of his coalition, and Abraham, at great cost to himself, says, "No! I won't keep the spoils. I won't be part of your coalition. I won't be that kind of man."

The other king, Melchizedek, is an intriguing character. He is mentioned only briefly. He is also called the priest of the Most High God. In other words, Abraham finds God at work in people from places he didn't even know about. In Genesis 14:18 we read that Melchizedek blessed Abram. Melchizedek let Abraham know that his victories and possessions were gifts from God and that they really didn't belong to Abraham.

What reality is there in your Christianity if you look at men struggling in darkness and you are content to congratulate yourselves that you are in the light?

FREDERICK WILLIAM ROBERTSON

LIFE APPLICATION | Tithing

We find an important biblical teaching introduced through the life of Abraham when we read, "Then Abram gave him a tenth of everything." The lesson of tithing (giving our first tenth) is significant because when we give, when we tithe, we are living in covenant relationship with the God who provides for his children. We declare boldly that we trust God to bless us, and we long for him to use us to be a blessing to others. That's what Abraham does here. He sets a standard we should all embrace.

INTERPRETIVE INSIGHT | Covenant Breakers and the Covenant Keeper

In Abraham's day, when somebody violated a covenant, it was not voided. It was not ripped up. When somebody violated a covenant, there were specific consequences. When this happened, things became very unpleasant for the violator. In most cases, blood was shed!

When we understand the cost of broken covenants in the Old Testament, we discover the power of Jesus' words when he said, "This cup is the new covenant *in my blood.*" The old covenant had been broken by sinful human beings. The covenant was violated. Somebody had to pay. Jesus said, "I'll pay. I'll suffer. I will pay the price that my children deserve, and then I will cut a new, unforgettable, and unshakable covenant with my blood. I will be cut. I will cut a covenant with my body." When we have this picture in our minds, coming to the communion table takes on a whole new level of significance. We realize that the punishment we deserve was paid by Jesus.

WORD STUDY
Theophany

The Old Testament is full of theophanies. These are manifestations of God's presence in a form that people can see and recognize. The burning bush is a great example. We need to note that in the Pentateuch, smoke and fire often symbolize the presence of God. So when the text says, "The fire and the torch passed between the pieces," we need to recognize that this is a picture of God. This visual appearance is what theologians call a *theophany*.

HISTORICAL CONTEXT | Cutting a Covenant

In most translations we read, "The LORD made a covenant." But in the Hebrew it literally says, "The LORD cut a covenant." The reason this term was used is both shocking and powerful!

In those days, when people made a covenant, they would take animals and literally cut them in two pieces and set the two pieces next to each other, side by side. Then they would go for a covenant walk. They would pass between the pieces of the animal, and the symbolic meaning of this walk was, "May this be my fate if I don't live up to the covenant, if I don't honor the covenant, if I am not faithful." Jeremiah 34:18 says, "Those who have violated my covenant, I will treat like the calf they cut in two and then walked between its pieces." When people cut a covenant, blood was shed. It was a way of saying, "I take this very seriously."

As we study God's covenant with Abraham, we need to notice who makes the covenant walk (Genesis 15:17). It is God! God is the one who passes between the dead carcasses of the animals—as if to say, "I will keep my agreement with you, and if I don't, may I be like these animals!" That's unbelievable! God condescends to take an oath. "Abram, I want so much for you to trust me, I'll take the covenant walk. May it be so with me if I don't keep my word to you." This is truly amazing!

DTR 3: The Call to Hope

God gave Abraham a specific and staggering promise. The promise was that Abraham would have descendants as vast as the stars in the heavens and as numerous as the sand on the seashore. The God who called Abraham to leave everything and to go to a new place had assured him that a new community would be born!

There was just one problem: Abraham had no descendants. He had no kids. What was worse, he was in his eighties, Sarah was in her seventies, and his wife was barren. Abraham and Sarah had a promise—but no children. They had a word from God in their hearts—but no baby in their arms.

Out of this painful and apparently hopeless situation God brings laughter, joy, and hope. As we look at this DTR moment in Abraham's life, we discover that God calls us to cling to hope even when outside circumstances dictate against it.

SIGNIFICANT SCRIPTURE

Genesis 16; 17:15-22; 18:9-15; 21:1-7

NARRATIVE ON THE TEXT | My Way

In Genesis 16 we discover that Sarah (Sarai) and Abraham know what it feels like to become hopeless. Although they were called to hope, they have grown discouraged. Sarah lets Abraham know that she feels the Lord has kept her from having children, so she is ready to institute her own plan: She will have children through Hagar. She actually tells Abraham to sleep with her servant Hagar and have children with her. Abraham agrees and does as Sarah requests.

This seems a little passive on Abraham's part. He doesn't argue real hard. As you read the passage, it is a little troubling. You can almost hear Abraham say, "Well, OK honey, if you think it's a good idea. I'll do it for you." Abraham follows through on his words, and Hagar conceives a little boy. Some time later, Ishmael is born.

This is a powerful example of trying to accomplish God's plan, but doing it my way!

ON THE LIGHTER SIDE | Cross My Heart

There is a small reflection of this kind of thinking in our day with children. When kids make a serious promise, they'll often say, "I promise. *Cross my heart and hope to die, stick a needle in my eye.*" This is a gruesome image, but it makes a point (pun intended). This is the way children say, "I'm really being truthful. I really honor my word. If I am lying, it will cost me!"

INTERPRETIVE INSIGHT | Another Fall

In his telling the story of Ishmael's conception and birth, we discover that the writer is very artistically crafting this passage by repeating the words from the Fall in the Garden of Eden. Back in the garden the writer said, "The woman took some [of the fruit] . . . and gave some to her husband." Literally the text says, "And the man listened to the voice of the woman." And here the writer says, "And Abram listened to the voice of Sarai. And Sarai took . . . Hagar . . . gave her to her husband to be his wife." It's another fall. This is not trusting covenant behavior! This is just another reminder of the reality of the Fall and the power of sin to break the community God wants to establish.

....

The Christian life that is joyless is
a discredit to God and a disgrace to itself.
MALTBIE D. BABCOCK

NARRATIVE ON THE TEXT | The Birth of Hope and Laughter

Genesis 18 and 21 are filled with hope and laughter. Visitors come and tell Abraham that Sarah will bear a child and the dream of a new community will be born. But we need to remember that Abraham is just shy of a hundred years old, and Sarah is now almost ninety. The childbearing years have come and gone for this couple . . . or so it would seem.

God speaks through three visitors who pay a visit to Abraham and Sarah, and Sarah is in the tent listening as the Lord is talking to Abraham. God promises that in a year Sarah will have a baby, their baby, in her arms. She cannot help herself; she lets out a muffled laugh at the very thought of herself and Abraham experiencing pregnancy and delivery at this stage in their life. Her response is recorded for us: "So Sarah laughed to herself as she thought, 'After I am worn out and my master is old, will I now have this pleasure?'"

Sarah may have been a little ironic in her choice of words. To her, the whole proposal must have sounded absurd. Abraham is ninety-nine years old and Sarah is eighty-nine. Viagra has not yet been invented! How could this be?

God asks Abraham why Sarah laughed. But Sarah lies and claims she did not laugh. In response, God assures her that she did laugh and that he heard her: "Yes, you did. You did too laugh. I heard you laugh." They have a little "did Sarah laugh?" debate right here.

As we move on, we see that Abraham and Sarah are filled with doubt, but they seek to obey God and live in a hope that seems beyond their reach. Finally, one day, a child is born. God tells them to name him Isaac. He is aptly named, because Isaac means, "He laughs."

DTR 4: A Call to Deeper Faith

As we look at the life of Abraham, it is clear that God is in the process of shaping a relationship. First he is called to leave everything he knows; this is a huge DTR moment. Next, God cuts a covenant with Abraham; this is a second DTR moment of epic proportions. Third, Abraham and Sarah are called to hope in a promise that has begun to feel hopeless. But as they seek to walk in faith and hope, God gives them a son.

We might wonder, isn't that enough? Haven't they grown to full maturity? Could there possibly be another DTR between God and this elderly couple? But we discover in Genesis 22 that the greatest challenge is still ahead! Just when you wonder if maybe you have grown all you can grow, God says, "Let's take another step of faith." Just when you think God cannot stretch you anymore, you discover that it is time for one more DTR!

INTERPRETIVE INSIGHT | This Is Just a Test!

Genesis 22:1 is an important first sentence. The writer wants us to know what Abraham does not know, namely, that what he will soon go through is only a test. The writer knows that the strain of this passage will be too intense for readers if they don't understand, in advance, that this is only a test. God is asking Abraham to take a shocking step of faith. "Will you trust me even when you don't understand? Even when it doesn't make sense?" God does not intend Abraham to kill Isaac; this option is never really on the table. But Abraham does not know this.

SIGNIFICANT SCRIPTURE

Genesis 22:1–18

NARRATIVE ON THE TEXT | A Hard Walk of Faith

God calls, "Abraham!" And Abraham says, "Here I am." We need to understand that when Abraham says this, he is not talking about his location. He is saying, "Speak, Lord. Whatever you say I will do. I will obey. Here I am. I am your servant." All of his life, Abraham has heard this voice. He heard it many decades

ON THE LIGHTER SIDE | Everyone Gets a Laugh!

Isaac is born, and the laughter continues. "Sarah said, 'God has brought me laughter, and everyone who hears about this will laugh with me.'" She was right! People laughed at a child born in the geriatric ward, with Medicare picking up the tab. They laughed because Sarah is the only woman in the supermarket who's buying Pampers and Depends at the same time. People laugh when Sarah stocks up on strained vegetables for Isaac, Abraham, and herself because nobody in the family has a single tooth.

ago when it told him to leave his home . . . and he did. He'd heard it when it called him to be in a covenant relationship . . . and he accepted. This same God called Abraham to hope and trust for the son that seemed to be an impossible dream. Abraham trusted and God provided.

Now this voice speaks to Abraham one more time. It's the last time he hears God's voice in Scripture. God says, "Take your son, your only son, Isaac, whom you love" and sacrifice him! It is interesting to note that this is the first time the word "love" is used in the Bible. It's used for a father who is willing to sacrifice his beloved son.

We need to also remember that this is not just his son; rather, this son is the promise of a new community. This is the dream. There is nobody else to step in and take the role that has been assigned to Isaac.

Once again, Abraham obeys God's call. He and Isaac begin a three-day journey. The details in this story are almost excruciating. "On the third day Abraham looked up and saw the place in the distance." We read in Genesis 22:6 that he takes wood for the burnt offering and places it on his son Isaac. But Abraham carries the fire and the knife himself. Why does he do this? Because fire and a sharp knife are things that can hurt a young boy. So, instinctively, Abraham carries them to protect his son. What a dramatic contrast! While he is taking his son to a place he will be sacrificed, Abraham is looking out for his safety.

The strain becomes almost unbearable. In verse 7 Isaac says, "Father?"

"Yes, my son?"

"The fire and the wood are here, but where is the lamb for the burnt offering?"

Abraham assures him, "God will provide, my son."

Abraham keeps saying, "My son. My son." You can almost hear the grief in his voice.

Soon they arrive at the place of sacrifice. Abraham builds the altar . . . in obedience. He takes the wood off Isaac's back . . . in obedience. Now it is time. Abraham takes Isaac, the promise of the new community, the dream of God, and in obedience he prepares for the sacrifice. He ties up his legs and binds his arms so there will be no struggle at the end. He picks up his son, and he holds the same body that he held on the first day he came from Sarah's womb. This is the little body he used to bathe and rock and tell stories to about a home somewhere far behind him, and a greater home somewhere in the future—a home Abraham would never know, but maybe Isaac would.

He places Isaac on the altar.

NEW TESTAMENT CONNECTION

Mount Moriah

According to 2 Chronicles 3:1, Mount Moriah is the same mountain on which the temple was built—in essence, the same mountain on which Jesus was crucified, Mount Calvary. Many centuries later, God the Father did exactly as Abraham does here. He took his only Son, whom he loved (note God's words at Jesus' baptism and transfiguration, Mark 1:11; 9:7), put on him the wood (the cross), and, like Abraham, was fully intent on the death of his Son (cf. Acts 2:23, God's set purpose and foreknowledge caused him to be handed over to his enemies for crucifixion). This time, however, there was no substitute ram in the bushes. Jesus shed his own blood for us—the blood of the Son of God. In other words, God sacrificed his Son on Mount Moriah so that we might have life, so that we might be in covenant (the new covenant) with him.

As he looks at Isaac, he remembers that this is the little body he would check on at night to make sure it was still breathing. This was the boy named "laughter," whom he had held countless times and chuckled to himself at the sheer impossibility of it all. But right now there was no laughter.

Abraham looks at his boy on the altar and realizes that Isaac is the reason he left everything so many years ago. This boy is the one hope for a multitude that will be formed into God's new community. This is his son, his only son, Isaac, whom he loves.

In obedience, Abraham takes the knife and reaches toward heaven as he prepares to destroy, with a single thrust, the life that he has helped to create.

Then God says, "Abraham! Abraham!"

And Abraham replies, "Here I am"—the same words as at the beginning of the story. "Here I am, God. Where else am I going to go? Who else am I going to turn to? Who else would I follow?" And God says, "Don't harm your son. I know now that you fear me, you honor me, you reverence me, and you trust me."

Abraham breathes again. He receives his son back, and the dream of God's new community continues.

> *He asks all,*
> *but He gives all.*
> THOMAS R. KELLY

INTERPRETIVE INSIGHT | A Vision of Hope

Abraham goes on to die a very old man. There's a poignant scene at his grave in Genesis 25:9. As we read about his burial, we see his sons Isaac *and* Ishmael there together. They are together for the first time since they were separated at Isaac's infancy. These two brothers whom God loved, whom God was with, are now together at their father's grave.

Our world still waits for the children of Isaac and the children of Ishmael to live together like brothers under the covenant of love. The world still waits for the day when bloodshed ends and the peace of God can reign.

HISTORICAL CONTEXT | The Value of Life

Among the many lessons we can learn from the story of Abraham and Isaac is that God does not affirm human sacrifice. In those days, many of the people in that region did offer their children as sacrifices. The Ammonites were known for their devotion to a false god they called Molech. They often sacrificed children to him. But God warned the people of Israel, "Do not give any of your children to be sacrificed to Molech, for you must not profane the name of your God. I am the LORD" (Leviticus 18:21). Unlike the false gods that were worshiped in that region, the God of Abraham would not tolerate human or infant sacrifice. Life is too sacred!

PAUSE FOR REFLECTION | An Invitation

At the end of the message, before you close in prayer, you might want to pause and invite those present to quiet their heart and reflect on one of the following questions. Take a moment for silence and allow room for the Holy Spirit to speak to the heart of each person.

- What do you need to *leave* behind if you are going to fully follow God?

- Are you walking in *covenant* relationship with God through Jesus? Are there any ways you are breaking the covenant?

- Where do you need to experience new *hope* in your life?

- What *step of faith* might you take today that will help you walk more closely with God?

God Is with Us

GENESIS 24:1-58; 27-33; 37; 39; 50:19-21

The Heart of the
MESSAGE

Have you ever noticed that you can be in a crowd of people and still feel very alone? We have all experienced moments of deep loneliness in this life. Even those extroverted people who seem to be the life of the party and always have someone calling them to "do lunch" or "meet for coffee" know what it is to feel alone.

In this session of the Old Testament Challenge we will discover that God is with us, no matter what we might feel about our human relationships. Through the book of Genesis we see God reminding his people of his presence and care for them. In the moments they feel most alone, abandoned, and fearful, they hear God's persistent reminder that he is with them.

The Heart of the
MESSENGER

As you prepare to bring this message, take time for personal reflection. Identify times you have felt very alone. How did you respond to these feelings? How did you experience the presence of God during these times of your life? It will be important for you to hold these experiences in your heart as you teach. As you speak about God's presence, even in the hardest of times and the strangest of places, be aware of whether you are living with a conviction that God is with you.

**Brief Message
OUTLINE**

1 God is with Isaac

2 God is with Jacob

3 God is with Joseph

Sermon Introduction

NARRATIVE ON LIFE | Looking at Genesis

One of the most ironic remarks people make about the Bible goes something like this: "The Bible is a book of pious, well-meaning advice that is not relevant to, or reflective of, the real world." People who make this kind of comment immediately betray one simple fact: They haven't actually read the Bible. If we are honest, a simple reading of the book of Genesis will show that the Bible pulls no punches and glosses over nothing. It is real life, down to earth, and relevant to the point of being startling.

If you read the book of Genesis, the number of mixed-up families you meet will shock you. Here is a quick overview:

- Cain is jealous of his brother Abel and kills him.
- Lamech introduces polygamy to the world.
- Noah, the most righteous man of his generation, gets drunk and curses his grandson.
- Lot, when his home is surrounded by the residents of Sodom who want to violate his visitors, offers his daughters instead.
- Later on, Lot's daughters get him drunk and get impregnated by him, and we are told that Lot is the "most righteous man in Sodom."
- Abraham plays favorites between his sons Isaac and Ishmael, and they end up estranged from each other.
- Isaac plays favorites between his sons, Jacob and Esau, and they become bitter enemies for twenty years.
- Jacob plays favorites between Joseph and his eleven other sons, and they want to kill him but end up selling him as a slave to travelers from another country.

The marriages in the book of Genesis are filled with disaster.

- Abraham has sex with his wife's servant (at his wife's request) and then he sends her and their son off into the desert.
- Isaac and Rebekah fight over which of their boys is going to get the blessing.
- Jacob marries two wives and ends up in a fertility contest with both his wives and their maids.
- Jacob's firstborn son, Reuben, sleeps with his father's concubine.

- Another one of Jacob's sons, Judah, sleeps with his daughter-in-law (she is disguised as a prostitute and he does not know who she is).

These people are badly messed up. These are not the Waltons! They need Dr. Phil, Dr. Laura, Dr. Ruth, Dr. Spock, Dr. Seuss—they need somebody!

INTERPRETIVE INSIGHT | Why Be So Honest?

When we begin reading the Old Testament, we are quickly convinced that these are not a bunch of pious stories that look nothing like real life. The opposite is true. When we begin to read the Bible, we start to wonder why the writer includes so much graphic detail about the sins and real-life struggles of these people. Why is all this shocking material here?

Some of these stories are indeed shocking and horrific. For instance, Genesis 34 tells the story of Jacob's daughter, Dinah. She is raped by a man named Shechem, but her father is passive; he does nothing to vindicate her. However, the sons of Jacob respond by telling the men of Shechem's city that if they get circumcised, they will be welcome to marry the women of Israel. The men of the city agree, and they are all circumcised. While they are in great pain after their surgery (remember, this was done with flint knives and no anesthetic), Levi and Simeon enter the city and murder all of them!

The behavior of all the men in this story is a disgrace, but the writer of Genesis never says, "Here's the bad guy" or "Here's the moral of the story." It can leave the reader wondering, "What's going on?"

To start with, it is critical that we recognize that the author of Genesis is not morally confused. The Pentateuch is the source of the Ten Commandments. These opening five books of the Bible are the most morally influential writings in the history of the world. The Pentateuch is a work of an absolute genius.

What we need to realize is that the writer of Genesis is perfectly capable of saying, "You shall not murder. You shall not steal. You shall not commit adultery." And he does say those things. The Pentateuch is filled with moral absolutes. At the same time, the writer of Genesis tells stories to force us to think. When we read these stories, we have to develop discernment and apply judgment.

These stories are often a kind of moral case-study. They are quite complex, with real people in all of their ambiguity. The story of Dinah's rape and her brothers' revenge demands that the reader of Scripture ask questions like, "When something terrible happens, how do I distinguish between justice, which is good, and vengeance, which is death?" This question, which was relevant in the days of the Old Testament, is just as relevant today. God does not always give us an easy and clear answer, but he often invites us to use the mind he has given us to grapple with hard issues and come to godly conclusions.

INTERPRETIVE INSIGHT | The Real Hero

As we read through the opening book of the Bible, we discover that God does not always give us commentary on what we read. The good guys don't have a halo over their head and the bad guys don't have horns. Sometimes the good people make poor choices and enter into sin. At other times, a person who seems like the villain ends up doing something that honors God. In movies and books we can usually figure out fairly quickly who the hero is, but in the Pentateuch it can be hard to tell.

Why is this? Why are so many of the pivotal players such a mixture of strength and weakness? Why are so many of the stories in the Old Testament filled with people who seem so human? The reason is that these people are not to be held up as the heroes in the story. Certainly we can learn a great deal from Abraham and Sarah, but they are not the heroes. There is no question that Joseph's life-lessons are there to teach us about faithfulness and endurance, but he is not to be exalted as the final hero in the story.

The stories recorded in the Bible are there to point us to the real hero—God. God is working with real flesh-and-blood people. God knows that these people are living in a terribly fallen world and that sin does unspeakable damage. So God sheds light on what people are really like, but also on what he is like. At the end of the day, we all need to discover that God is the hero and that each of these stories points us toward him!

1. God Is with Isaac

It is easy to believe God cares about the big things in the world. International crises, the decisions of presidents, kings and queens, world hunger, and the spread of the Gospel—these are the things that must occupy the heart of God. We have no problem being confident that God wants to be involved in the big things that happen in this world.

But what about the little stuff? Is God available to help with my personal needs? For instance, does God care enough to get involved in helping me figure out the right career? Is he concerned about helping me choose healthy friends? Does God care enough to get involved in the process of helping me find the right person to marry? As we look at the life of Isaac, we discover that God not only cares deeply about the details of our lives, he wants to get intimately involved with us. God is with us in the big things of life, and he is also with us in the little things.

SIGNIFICANT SCRIPTURE

Genesis 24:1–58

NARRATIVE ON THE TEXT | God Is with Isaac

Isaac discovered that God was with him in a unique way. It came through the provision of a wife, through an amazing series of circumstances. Abraham was growing old. He had experienced great blessing and provision from the hand of God. His son Isaac was drawing near the age when he would marry, but Abraham was concerned about who his wife would be. Thus, he called his chief servant in for an important meeting. We know that Eliezer was Abraham's chief servant over all of his affairs, so we can be fairly confident that this was the one who carried out Abraham's plan. When Eliezer entered the room, Abraham asked him to place his hand under his thigh and swear by the Lord that he would do what Abraham was about to request.

INTERPRETIVE INSIGHT | What's Wrong with a Canaanite Woman?

What would have been so bad if Isaac had married a Canaanite woman? What was the big deal? Abraham's concern here is that Isaac will not be tempted into idolatry—into leaving this God of the covenant. Abraham knows the potential lure of love. If Isaac were to marry a pagan, Canaanite woman, he might just end up worshiping her false gods and dishonoring the one true God.

LIFE APPLICATION | Being Equally Yoked

The warning we see here in Genesis about the danger of marrying somebody who is not committed to God runs all the way through the whole Old Testament and into the New Testament. In numerous places in the Old Testament, God warns against intermarrying with the pagan nations (for example, see Exodus 34:15–16; Deuteronomy 7:3; Ezra 9–10). Paul talks about the importance of being "equally yoked" (2 Corinthians 6:14). Because God's people are part of a covenant community, they should marry people who are also followers of Christ.

Note to the teacher. It is helpful for you as a teacher/preacher to remind God's people of this important biblical truth. We live in a day when many followers of Christ are asking if it is really a big deal if they marry someone who is not a fully devoted follower of Jesus. The answer is the same today as it was the day Abraham sent Eliezer to find a wife for Isaac.

HISTORICAL CONTEXT | Just Part of the Oath

In our day and age, we tend to seal an agreement with a handshake. This works quite well for most people. But in Abraham's day, the tradition was different.

Placing a hand under a person's thigh was just part of the oath. It would have been as natural as shaking hands in our day. It was a method of promise in the old days, an expression of complete trust. In

this oath, Eliezer promises that he will not get a wife for Isaac from the daughters of the Canaanites. Rather, he will find a wife for Isaac among Abraham's own people.

NARRATIVE ON THE TEXT | Eliezer on a Mission

Abraham sends his chief-of-staff, Eliezer, off with a caravan of ten camels loaded down with all sorts of riches and provisions. Anyone who saw this caravan coming would know that someone with great wealth was coming to town.

We need to understand the difficult nature of this assignment. Eliezer is sent to a part of the world he doesn't know, and there are no maps to show him the way. He has to find Abraham's relatives and talk them into sending one of their women away forever to marry some kid they've never met. From the very beginning, this is a huge challenge.

It is a joy to see what Eliezer does first. He prays, "O LORD, God of my master Abraham, give me success today, and show kindness to my master Abraham" (Genesis 24:12). Eliezer prays. This is only the second prayer recorded in the entire Bible. The first one is when Abraham intercedes on behalf of Sodom and Gomorrah.

Eliezer is not a part of Abraham's lineage, though he is a part of the circumcised covenant community and he does trust God. This servant calls out to the God of Abraham. If you look closely, you will see a detail that some people might miss. While Eliezer is still praying, while he is still on his knees, while he is in the process of asking for the right woman to come along so that Isaac might have a wife, Rebekah walks onto the scene.

Eliezer meets Rebekah, and she exceeds his prayer. She is a relative of Abraham, as he has prayed. This is good news because she'll be less likely to tempt her husband Isaac to worship idols. She's also available to be a wife because she is a virgin; moreover, she is "very beautiful." What more could Isaac (and Abraham) ask for?

> *The smallest act of kindness is better than the greatest of kind intentions.*
>
> KEN GIRE

HISTORICAL CONTEXT | Thirsty

A thirsty camel can drink up to thirty gallons of water. Simple math shows that Rebekah was offering to draw up to three hundred gallons of water, since there were ten camels.

When we think about getting water, we imagine turning a knob and watching the water flow. In those days, the wells were often deep. The water was retrieved by throwing a bucket down the well and pulling it up by hand. To draw three hundred gallons of water by hand was a task that would exhaust most people, then or now. Yet Rebekah gladly offers to do this humble act of service. In this story we learn a couple of things about Rebekah. First, she has a servant's heart. Second, this girl has some serious biceps!

LIFE APPLICATION | The Power of Specific Prayers

Eliezer discovers the power of prayer in a big way! He has asked the God of Abraham to send along a woman who will be willing to water all ten of his camels after their long and arid trip. In response to his prayer, Rebekah arrives and offers to do exactly what Eliezer prayed.

For Eliezer, a specific prayer leads to a specific answer. Too often we offer up vague prayers. In many cases, our prayers can be so general that we have no idea if they are actually answered. We need to learn to be specific in our prayer requests. There is no guarantee that every prayer we lift up will be answered in the affirmative. But when a prayer is answered, we should be able to recognize it because the request has been specific.

NARRATIVE ON THE TEXT | Rebekah's Decision

Rebekah's response and dramatic act of service is even more impressive because we know she doesn't have any idea what's at stake. She doesn't know that her whole future and participation in God's redemptive community is on the line. She is just serving.

Eliezer recognizes that God is at work in this far country. He sees that this beautiful, servant-hearted woman is the answer to his prayer. Eliezer gives her some expensive jewelry as a gift from Abraham and Isaac, and Rebekah invites him to meet her family. Eliezer knows it is going to take a fair amount of ingenuity and wise persuasion on his part, but he has no question that God is at work.

Eliezer meets Rebekah's brother Laban and quickly discovers what makes him tick. He is a money guy (we will discover this in greater detail in the next OTC message). He is very interested in money, and the costly jewelry Rebekah is wearing gets Laban's attention.

Within a short time, Eliezer clearly expresses why he has come and tells them the whole story of his bold and specific prayer as well as Rebekah's actions that fulfilled his prayer. Eliezer asks if Rebekah can go with him immediately. When she is asked if she is willing to accompany Eliezer back so that she can meet Isaac and become his wife, she responds with one word (in the Hebrew) that simply means, "I will go." Eliezer has accomplished his mission, and he is ready to head home.

NEW TESTAMENT CONNECTION

Ask, Seek, and Knock!

Jesus was the wisest man who ever lived. Here is what he had to say in Luke 11:9–13 about the Father's desire to hear and answer our prayers:

"So I say to you: Ask and it will be given to you; seek and you will find; knock and the door will be opened to you. For everyone who asks receives; he who seeks finds; and to him who knocks, the door will be opened.

"Which of you fathers, if your son asks for a fish, will give him a snake instead? Or if he asks for an egg, will give him a scorpion? If you then, though you are evil, know how to give good gifts to your children, how much more will your Father in heaven give the Holy Spirit to those who ask him!"

Deism and Pantheism

The theologians are right when they say God is transcendent. But if people believe in a God who is *only* transcendent, they end up adopting what's called *deism*. The idea of deism is that God created the world and then decided to have little or nothing to do with it. God got the ball rolling, but now it is up to us. God has no plans to meddle, interfere, or help.

The other extreme is the belief that God is *only* immanent and not transcendent. This leads to something called *pantheism*. This is a belief that God is so immanent that material things are divine. These philosophies and religious systems lead people to worship the earth, the sun, and the moon.

LIFE APPLICATION | Beginning with Prayer and Ending with Praise

Eliezer began his task with a clear and specific prayer. What a wonderful example for all of us. He was facing a challenge and knew he could never accomplish it on his own, so he prays.

When his task is completed successfully, he bows down again and lifts up a prayer of praise. Note Genesis 24:27: "Then the man bowed down and worshiped the LORD, saying, 'Praise be to the LORD, the God of my master Abraham, who has not abandoned his kindness and faithfulness to my master. As for me, the LORD has led me on the journey to the house of my master's relatives.'"

Eliezer is given a difficult assignment. He begins in prayer. He sees God work. Finally, he ends with worship. This is a God thing every step of the way! Eliezer becomes an example of how we should live our lives: Begin with prayer and end with praise. What a great model for life!

INTERPRETIVE INSIGHT | A New Vision of God

The writer of Genesis is saying something unprecedented. This had never been said before to the history of the human race. Genesis is teaching us that the one and only transcendent God, who existed before time, who was in the beginning, who created the heavens and the earth, is also the immanent God who is with us right here, right now. In this story we discover that the transcendent Creator of the heavens and earth is concerned about nomads, their kids, and a servant named Eliezer. In this story we see God revealing himself as both transcendent and immanent.

WORD STUDY | Transcendent, Immanent, and Omnipresence

For centuries Christian theologians have used three words to describe God. One of them is *transcendence*. Our God, the God of the Bible, is a transcendent God. The idea behind this word is that God is eternally self-sufficient apart from his creation. He was around way before the world was created. He can live apart from his creation. Isaiah 6:1 gives us a picture of this: "I saw the Lord seated on the throne, high and exalted." God is totally other from us. He is the infinite and holy God.

A second word theologians use to describe God, which is a sort of counterpoint to transcendence, is *immanence*. The idea of immanence is that God is continuously, actively present with us. This theological concept is similar to the idea of the next word, though with a subtle difference. Immanence means God is active everywhere. God sees. God knows. God cares. God works.

Omnipresence is a spatial concept, which teaches us that God is everywhere. The psalmist paints a picture of God's omnipresence with these words: "If I go up to the heavens, you are there; if I make my bed in the depths, you are there" (Psalm 139:8). Wherever I go, God, you are there with me.

He is the God Immanuel, which means "God with us." He's the God who is next to us every moment of every day. This transcendent God is present and intimately concerned about the little details of our daily lives. Isaac discovered this powerful spiritual reality and lived in it through his whole life, and so can we.

2. God Is with Jacob

There are people in this world who never seem to learn from their mistakes. Because they refuse to learn, they are doomed to repeat the same unhealthy behaviors over and over again. There are also people who *do* learn from their mistakes. These people grow in wisdom and avoid all sorts of pain and struggle. However, there is a group of people who are wisest of all. These are the men and women who learn from the mistakes of others. They watch, listen, and learn. Rather than having to face the consequences of unwise choices and actions, they see the results of these things in the lives of others and avoid them at all costs.

The story of Jacob's life is an example of all three of these kinds of people wrapped into one. Sometimes when we look at Jacob, we see a man who repeats the same mistakes over and over. At other times, Jacob learns from his mistakes and grows in maturity as he discovers that God is with him, even in the hard times. As we walk through Jacob's life, we see him grow in wisdom and come to a place where he is able to learn from the mistakes of others and not have to feel pain before he learns the lessons God wants to teach him. As we study the life of Jacob, we are invited to a place of wisdom where we can discover God's desire to be with us and teach us in every experience of life.

NARRATIVE ON THE TEXT | Jacob the Deceiver

Isaac and Rebekah are married and God's plan of community continues. They end up having twin sons, Jacob and Esau. Jacob is a con artist. He is a scammer. Jacob is always looking for an angle, and he's like that right out of the womb.

Genesis 25:24–26 tells the story of the birth of this odd couple. Esau was the firstborn, and this kid had a serious hair problem. The Bible tells us that when he was born, he was like a hairy garment. Jacob came next, and when he came out he was grasping onto his brother's heel.

WORD STUDY

Jacob and Esau— What's in a Name?

Both of these boys receive names that fit them. *Esau* simply means "red." One obvious reason for this name is that he was a redhead—and a red everything else. This kid has red hair from head to toe! Also, later in life, he sells his birthright to his brother for a bowl of red stew.

Jacob literally means "he who grasps the heel." Metaphorically his name meant "the deceiver." Jacob's name is a foreshadowing of the kind of character Jacob will have for a good portion of his life. Jacob becomes the one who grasps the heel, the one who trips others up, the deceiver. But with time, God will give him a new name and a new character.

SIGNIFICANT SCRIPTURE

Genesis 27-33

NARRATIVE ON THE TEXT | Messed-Up Family Dynamics

As these two boys grow up, they become two dramatically different people. Esau is a hunter and an outdoorsman. Jacob is a quiet man who likes to stay inside. We read that, again, the parents make the mistake of playing favorites. Isaac dotes over Esau because he is a jock; he's a man's man. This kid might not be the brightest lightbulb on the chandelier, and he might have some serious body hair, but he also has the heart and affection of his father.

Rebekah favors Jacob. She helps Jacob trick his dad into stealing the family blessing from Esau. She teaches her boy how to be Jacob the deceiver. You don't have to look hard to discover that you have some really messed-up family dynamics here. Things get so bad that when Esau realizes he has lost both his birthright and blessing to his younger brother, he plans to kill him.

LIFE APPLICATION | No Favorites

All through the book of Genesis we see examples of parents playing favorites. Here is the key observation we need to make. It never works out well. There is never a sense that these actions and attitudes of favoritism bring life and health. They never lead to the edification of the children or the parents. Favoritism brings conflict, tension, and brokenness in each family.

What a sobering reminder to all those gathered who are parents or hope to be parents. It is also a good warning to grandparents and other family members, like aunts and uncles. Beware of the danger of favoritism. God's Word teaches some good lessons about avoiding favoritism. Many of those gathered have experienced the sting of growing up in a home where they were not "the favorite." God longs that this dysfunction not be passed on to the next generation.

NARRATIVE ON THE TEXT | Jacob on the Run

As the story of Jacob and Esau continues, God decides Jacob must go to character school. Life is going to get very hard for Jacob. He will have to travel a long way from home. But God wants Jacob to know he is not abandoned. God is still with him. When we get to Genesis 28, Jacob has left his home and is fleeing from his brother, Esau. Jacob runs for his life, but he has no idea that he is running straight toward the arms of the God who is with him and into the plans God has for him.

While on the run, Jacob has a vision. This is one of the most important visions of the Old Testament. In this vision, Jacob comes to see that God is present with him.

PAUSE FOR REFLECTION

Being Aware

Where is the house of God? Where is God present? Everywhere. He is right next to each one of us. So often we are like Jacob and have to say—"Surely the Lord is in this place, and I was not aware of it." Our goal should be to grow in our awareness of God's presence and become people who can say, "Surely the Lord is in this place and I see it. I see him at work."

It could be a very rich experience to take a few moments of silence and invite those gathered to reflect on life situations where God is present, but they are not tuned in to see and hear him. Invite the Holy Spirit to speak to the heart of each person and begin to give them a greater clarity to realize that God is with them, even in the times and places he is hard to recognize.

INTERPRETIVE INSIGHT | Jacob's Ladder

In Jacob's vision he sees a kind of a staircase with angels of God ascending and descending from heaven. This is the kingdom of heaven intersecting with earth and human life. God is present and is speaking to Jacob. This is one of the most fundamental visions any human being has ever had because it gives a picture of the connectedness of the kingdom of heaven and those who dwell on this earth. In this vision, Jacob is reminded that the transcendent God is also immanent.

Through this vision God is telling Jacob, "I am with you and will watch over you wherever you go, and I will bring you back to this land. I will not leave you until I have done what I have promised" (Genesis 28:15). What a life-changing reminder! When Jacob wakes up from his sleep and the vision is over, he realizes, "Surely the LORD is in this place, and I was not aware of it" (28:16). Jacob realizes something that we all need to discover at some point in our spiritual journey: God can be very present, and we can miss it. We need to pay attention and learn to see how God is with us at all times and in all places.

> *All God's giants have been weak people who did great things for God because they reckoned on his being with them.*
>
> J. HUDSON TAYLOR

NARRATIVE ON THE TEXT | New Family Ties

As we continue to study Jacob's life, we see the process of Jacob's transformation. In chapter 29 he goes to Haran, the hometown of his grandfather Abraham. Jacob travels hundreds of miles from Canaan to Haran, and there he meets his Uncle Laban. Jacob does not realize it right away, but when he meets Laban, he has met his match when it comes to deception. Laban is the king of con artists, and Jacob will learn some powerful life lessons as he relates to Laban in the coming years.

HISTORICAL CONTEXT | Big Rock

The stones that covered wells in those days were enormous. They weighed hundreds of pounds. They were designed to require several large, burly shepherds to remove them because they were supposed to protect the water supply, which was very precious. The whole idea of covering the well with such a big rock was to make sure that no one could uncover the well until all the shepherds arrived and moved the stone as a group. The sight of seeing one man move this rock would have been shocking.

WORD STUDY
Bethel

Jacob is learning that God is always intersecting with human life. In response, Jacob gets up early in the morning and sets up a pillar, a visual reminder of what he has learned. He pours oil on it and gives that place a new name. Before, it was called Luz. Now it will be called "Bethel." The name Bethel comes from two words: *beth*, which is the Hebrew word meaning "house," and *el*, a Hebrew word for God. This is "the house of God." This is the place where God is present.

When Jacob arrives in Haran, he meets some folks around a well. While he is talking with them, a beautiful shepherdess arrives. In Genesis 29:9 we read, "While he was still talking with them, Rachel came with her father's sheep, for she was a shepherdess. When Jacob saw Rachel daughter of Laban, his mother's brother, and Laban's sheep, he went over and rolled the stone away from the mouth of the well and watered his uncle's sheep."

NARRATIVE ON THE TEXT | Leah, Not Rachel

Laban has two daughters. Leah is the older one, but Jacob is in love with Rachel. He is so crazy over Rachel that he works seven years to earn her hand in marriage. That was the agreement. That was the deal. But we read these words: "They seemed like only a few days to him because of his love for her" (Genesis 29:20). Jacob is one love-sick, desperate guy.

In verse 21 we read, "Then Jacob said to Laban, 'Give me my wife. My time is completed, and I want to lie with her.'" That sounds a little crass. Most fathers would not recommend this as the lead-in line for a man who is ready to marry his daughter. Jacob is messing with the wrong guy, and he is about to discover a whole new level of deception. Jacob had a college degree in deception, but Laban had a doctorate. On his wedding night, into his tent, wrapped in a veil, silent in the darkness, Laban sends in his first daughter, Leah.

NARRATIVE ON THE TEXT | The Deceiver Deceived

As anyone would guess, Jacob is not happy about his morning surprise. So Jacob says to Laban (verse 25), "What is this you have done to me? I served you for Rachel, didn't I? Why have you [it is important to note the next word] deceived me?" The word he uses is a form of his own name—Jacob. And this is a theme in his story. In a sense, Jacob is asking Laban, "Why have you treated me the way I have treated so many others?"

ON THE LIGHTER SIDE | Love Steroids

Jacob, you'll remember, was an indoor boy. He was not a jock. He did not have the "Body by Jake." He had a body by Jacob, and it was not real impressive. It was Esau who loved to take off his shirt and flex his hairy biceps. But Jacob is so inspired by Rachel that he wants to show off. It's like he's all of a sudden on love steroids. Jacob, the indoor boy, puts his shoulder against this massive rock and pushes for all he is worth. To the surprise of everyone there, including Jacob, the stone rolls away.

INTERPRETIVE INSIGHT | I've Been Jacobed!

Later on in Genesis 31:7, Jacob says, "Laban deceived me by changing my wages ten times." The writer is telling us, with this kind of code word, that Jacob is now on the receiving end of what he had been dishing out his whole life. He has to learn what it feels like to be deceived. In the Hebrew, Jacob is actually asking Laban, "Why have you Jacobed me?" He has been out-deceived, and Jacob does not like it.

NARRATIVE ON THE TEXT | A Spiritual Overhaul

Jacob needs a spiritual overhaul. The road he will take to spiritual maturity will not be an easy one. He needs new eyes, a new mind, and a new heart. And there's no way to go through that process but the painful, laborious, character-building process of being on the receiving end for a while. Suffering will teach him what nothing else can. So he goes to Laban and asks, "Why have you deceived me?"

Laban informs Jacob of a painful reality, "It is not our custom here to give the younger daughter in marriage before the older one." Laban is getting in a dig. "Around here," he's saying, "we don't allow the grabby, younger child to steal the rights of an older one. You know of any cases where that happened? Maybe it's different where you come from, Jacob. But around here that sort of thing just doesn't fly."

NARRATIVE ON LIFE | The Story of the Unloved Sister

Think of what the wedding night must have been like for Leah. So often we tend to focus on Jacob and Rachel, but Leah was a real person, with real feelings, who experienced real pain. This is her one and only wedding night, and she's in the tent because her husband thinks she's Rachael. She says nothing. All she had to do was say a word, and it would be over. She says nothing. Why? Maybe she's afraid of her father's anger. Maybe she feels she's unattractive and she'll never be loved. Maybe she's desperately in love with Jacob.

ON THE LIGHTER SIDE | "It Was Leah"

What follows in this account is told with some wit, artistic flair, and great economy of words. Jacob shares his night and bed with the veiled woman Laban sends into his tent. Jacob is elated! He has waited for seven years for this night. He believes it is his beloved Rachel. Then the sun rises and we read these words recorded in verse 25, "When morning came, there was Leah!" Oops!

This story of the heartache of the unloved sister is one of the saddest in Scripture. But we read that God hears and God cares. God notices the tears of Leah. God is with Leah in her pain and sorrow. He cares for her and gives her children. What a great reminder that God is not just with the key players in the story, he is with each person at his or her point of need!

NARRATIVE ON THE TEXT | A Time of Transformation

For twenty years Jacob goes to character school. Jacob the deceiver meets Laban and learns about the pain of deception, and he begins to change. God is with him. Then he finally decides to return home and face his brother Esau. This is a courageous decision because Jacob has been a runner and an avoider his whole life. But now he decides to go back and be reconciled to his brother or die trying. It's a courageous thing to do.

Jacob has a life-changing encounter with God on the way. Jacob, the man who had lived in deceit, manipulation, and fear, wrestles all night with a man. Jacob says, "I will not let you go until you bless me" (Genesis 32:26). He discovers he is wrestling with God, and God says, "I'm going to give you a new name."

INTERPRETIVE INSIGHT | A New Man

After wrestling with God and receiving a new name, Israel is a different person. Before all this happened, he had devised a strategy to send groups ahead of him to try to meet Esau first and appease him. He had planned to let a series of gifts act as a buffer before he met his brother. Remember, last time these two brothers were together, Esau wanted him dead!

Before, Jacob fled in fear, but now he is Israel. He gathers his family and all he has and walks toward his brother. But instead of sending waves of animals, servants, and gifts ahead of him, we read these words, "He himself went on ahead." He's the fighter. He's going first. He's leading the way. He'll take the risk. He's a new man.

WORD STUDY

Israel

For a long portion of his life, the name of the man we have been studying was Jacob, the deceiver, and he lived out the meaning of his name. Now God gives him a new name, *Israel*. This new name points to his future. His new name means, "he who struggles with God."

NEW TESTAMENT CONNECTION

New Beginnings

In 2 Corinthians 5:17 the apostle Paul reminds us that God still brings new beginnings for each person who has a relationship with him through Jesus. Listen to these words: "Therefore, if anyone is in Christ, he is a new creation; the old has gone, the new has come!" The same God that made Jacob into Israel can give us a new beginning today!

LIFE APPLICATION | The Hope of Reconciliation

As we read the story, we might expect Esau to come with anger and vengeance. We read that he arrives to meet Jacob with four hundred men! This could have felt very threatening. But here we read some of the most touching words in the Bible: "But Esau ran to meet Jacob and embraced him; he threw his arms around his neck and kissed him. And they wept." And the long, slow, redemptive work of God bears fruit, and the dream of community wins a little bit. Finally, in this sad book, two brothers are reconciled.

3. God Is with Joseph

It is easy to recognize the presence of God in our lives when things are going well. When the sun is shining, there is money in the bank account, and our body feels healthy, there is a sense that God is near. But what about on the cloudy days, when the stock market does poorly, the doctor brings bad news, and relationships seem to be coming apart at the seams? Where is God when pain and sorrow envelop our lives? From Joseph we learn that God is still with us, even in the times of greatest darkness. And, sometimes, we find that God is with us in these times most of all.

PAUSE FOR REFLECTION

Broken Relationships

In light of this staggering example of reconciliation, this might be a good time to challenge people to identify a relationship where they need reconciliation. Give a word of hope and encouragement that God does have the power to restore even the most broken of relationships. Then allow a time of silence for people to invite the Holy Spirit to help them identify a relationship that needs healing.

HISTORICAL CONTEXT | Seeing Your Face

One of the great statements in the Bible is found in Genesis 33:10. This is definitely a verse worth underlining in your Bible. Jacob says to Esau, "If I have found favor in your eyes, accept this gift from me. For to see your face is like seeing the face of God."

Now, "to see the face" in the Hebrew language meant to know someone, to grasp their character. If you think about someone whose back is turned toward you, you can't see his or her character. But when they turn so you can see their face, you get to know their heart. You know what's going on inside of them. You see their face.

Israel is stumbling slowly toward knowing more and more about God.

As he grows to know God, it changes the way he sees people. So he says to his brother, Esau, "When you offer mercy, when you desire to reconcile, it reminds me of God. You remind me of God." The image of God begins to be a little more visible in human beings. It's just a beautiful statement: "For to see your face is like seeing the face of God."

SIGNIFICANT
SCRIPTURE

Genesis 37; 39; 50:19–21

INTERPRETIVE INSIGHT | Not a Perfect Son or Brother

Some people present Joseph as the perfect son who is treated badly by his brothers with no apparent provocation. But if you read this account carefully, it appears Joseph does not help things very much. The text suggests that he is a pretty spoiled kid and that he doesn't seem to mind it too much.

To get a sense of the family dynamics, we are told in Genesis 37:2, "Joseph, a young man of seventeen, was tending the flocks with his brothers, the sons of Bilhah and the sons of Zilpah, his father's wives, and he brought their father a *bad report* about them." Remember that Joseph is the son of Jacob's favorite wife, Rachel. These other boys are not Jacob's favorites. On top of this, Joseph brings a bad report about his brothers.

In our day, a kid who tells on his brothers and sisters is called a tattletale. This is actually somewhat worse. The word for "report" or "tale" used here occurs elsewhere in the negative sense of an untrue story. And here it is described by the word "bad" or "evil," which most likely means that Joseph made up bad stuff about his brothers, which was not entirely true, and his father believed him rather than his brothers.

HISTORICAL CONTEXT | A Lot More Than a Robe

Jacob, the father, gave Joseph a special robe. The adjective to describe it is a little uncertain in Hebrew. The NIV translates it "a robe with long sleeves." In the King James Version, the expression is a "coat of many colors." Though we don't know exactly what the robe looked like, we do have a sense of its significance.

Let's put it this way, Jacob got it from Nordstroms. It was hand-tailored. The rest of the boys got their clothes off the rack from K-Mart when the blue light was flashing. There is no question this coat set young Joseph apart from his brothers in a way that everyone could see. What made this coat explosive was not just that it was more expensive or made of nicer material. The problem was the meaning behind Jacob's giving this coat to his second youngest son (the older son of his favorite wife, Rachel).

There was a ceremony involving such robes in the ancient Near East that marked the recipient as the father's primary heir. Joseph, the eleventh son in the family lineage, takes the rights of the firstborn. Joseph gets the farm. When he receives this special robe, the situation is packed with emotions because the whole family inheritance is at stake. This is a volatile moment because the older boys can clearly see that Joseph has been placed before all of them. This is a recipe for sibling civil war, and that is exactly what happens.

NARRATIVE ON THE TEXT | A Look at Dreams

As we move on in the story, Joseph has a pair of dreams. Dreams were generally considered prophetic in those days, though, interestingly, here the writer does not say they are from God. He just leaves it open-ended. You would think Joseph might have the common sense to keep his dreams to himself. His brothers already have real problems with this fancy robe-wearing, inheritance-stealing younger brother.

Instead of having the wisdom to remain quiet, Joseph gathers all of his brothers together to tell them about his dream. Remember, these are the brothers who have no robe, who have been desperately hurt by their father, and who hate Joseph's guts. But he gathers them together and says, "Listen to my dream, brothers. In my dream all of you are little sheaves. And I am a great big sheaf. My sheaf rose up, and it stood tall, and your little sheaves gathered around and bowed down to my sheaf—which means one day I will rule over all of you." You can almost hear Joseph telling them, "I will command and you will submit. You will bow down in humble expression of your obedience to my authority. Isn't that cool? Aren't you happy about this dream? Let's play 'Bow Down Sheaf' now, just to get ready."

Their response is clear. Verse 4 says, "When his brothers saw that their father loved him more than any of them, they hated him and could not speak a kind word to him. Joseph had a dream, and when he told it to his brothers, they hated him all the more." Verse 8: "His brothers said to him, 'Do you intend to reign over us? Will you actually rule us?' And they hated him all the more because of his dream."

One word keeps popping up through this section of Genesis: "hate." In verse 9, Joseph has another dream. You'd think by now he'd learn to keep his dreams to himself. These dreams are not helping the family out. This time there are eleven stars, the sun, and the moon, and they all bow down to Joseph. Again, the brothers get the message loud and clear. This time they are being told that all of them, and their parents, will bow down to Joseph. Now they hate him even more! They hate him so much that they end up secretly selling him as a slave to a band of travelers heading to Egypt, and they tell his father that his favorite son is dead.

INTERPRETIVE INSIGHT | Character School

Jacob thinks Joseph is dead, but he is actually on his way to character school down in Egypt. Joseph had dreams of being exalted, but now he is a slave. This young man has gone from being on top of the pile to the bottom of the totem pole. But, even in slavery, betrayed by his brothers and taken against his will to a foreign country, we read these words, "The LORD was with Joseph" (Genesis 39:2).

Joseph arrives in Egypt and becomes a slave in the home of a wealthy leader named Potiphar. Things go pretty well until Mrs. Potiphar makes advances on Joseph and he rejects her. In retaliation, she lies and says he has assaulted her. Joseph ends up in prison because of that lie. All he has done is seek to honor God and remain faithful, and now he is being punished. At this point it would be easy for Joseph to feel he has been completely abandoned by God. But Genesis 39:20–21 says, "Joseph's master took him and put him in prison, the place where the king's prisoners were confined. But while Joseph was there in prison, the LORD was with him."

Joseph, who had been preoccupied with his own little dreams at home, now learns to notice and care for other prisoners. His physical living space has gotten much smaller, but his world has expanded. This moment marks the beginning of Joseph's exaltation. It's an interesting thing that Jacob, who was a deceiver, had to learn what it felt like to be deceived. Joseph, who dreamed of life at the top and spoke about it in grandiose terms, has to experience life at the bottom. It is precisely at the moments of his greatest pain and aloneness that God is with him.

From this place of darkness and imposed humility, God raises Joseph up and uses him to save whole populations in Egypt from starvation during a famine. Joseph is raised up through interpreting a series of dreams, and he becomes the second most powerful man in all of Egypt. Next to Pharaoh, Joseph rules over Egypt. One day, many years later, he is reconciled with his brothers.

INTERPRETIVE INSIGHT | Trusting God

Genesis 50:20 is a summary of Joseph's entire life. In a sense, it is a statement about the theology of Genesis. This short verse hits on a key Old Testament theme that helps us understand that God is at work and is with us even when we don't know it. When Joseph's brothers finally realize who he is, they throw themselves before him and tell him, "We'll be your slaves." They are sure he's furious at them. But he says, "Don't be afraid. I'm not angry with you. I'm not going to pronounce judgment on you."

God's love is more concerned with the development of a person's character than with the promotion of his or her comfort.
J. IRELAND HASLER

As they tremble in fear, knowing he can speak one word and have them executed for what they did to him so many years before, Joseph speaks these words, "You intended to harm me, but God intended it for good to accomplish what is now being done, the saving of many lives." Joseph realizes that the Lord God has been with him every step of the way!

LIFE APPLICATION | A God Hunt

Here's the assignment for all those who want to experience God's presence in deeper ways. We need to go on a God hunt.

David Mains used to talk about this idea on a radio show called "Chapel of the Air." A God hunt is simply learning to look for signs that the God who walked with Adam and Eve, with Enoch and Noah, with Abraham and Isaac and Jacob and Joseph really will be with us. If we learn to do this, it will make a fundamental difference in our lives. We begin to live with a new kind of expectancy.

Invite people to hunt for God in their daily lives. Here are five things they can look for. All of these come from the life experience of the three men we have studied in this session:

1. Concrete answers to specific prayers

2. Leadings or promptings from God

3. Unexpected resources

4. Surprising outcomes

5. God-ordained "demotions"

Each of these can help us see that God is with us, leading and shaping us each and every day.

God the Deliverer

EXODUS 1–12

The Heart of the
MESSAGE

Everyone faces moments in life when they need some help. Sometimes we humbly accept a hand from someone else. At other times, we stubbornly insist on doing things ourselves. Like the man or woman driving late at night who is hopelessly lost, we refuse to stop and ask for directions. We would rather stay lost than admit we need help. We have the strangest ability to live in the worst of situations and pretend everything is under control. Life goes so much better when we can admit we need help. All of us face moments when we need a deliverer.

The people of Israel came to this place often. Sometimes they stubbornly refused God's help and lived with the consequences. At other times they would cry out and accept God's delivering hand. All of us can grow to see God as our deliverer. Not only does he have the power to save, but also he longs to deliver his children. He is waiting to act. In this message we will discover how we can walk in the delivering power of God.

The Heart of the
MESSENGER

We all need the deliverance that only God can offer. The starting point is when we come to a place where we realize our sin has us captive and only God can save us through the shed blood of Jesus, the new Passover Lamb. As a leader in Christ's church, you have come to this place of calling on God for deliverance. As you prepare to bring this message, take time to thank God for sending his only Son as your deliverer.

However, God's delivering power and plans don't stop at the cross and the empty tomb. The same God who worked miracles in Egypt and parted the Red Sea is ready to move in your life today. As you are studying and preparing for this message, take time to evaluate your life—your habits, attitudes, and motives— and look for areas you might need God's deliverance. Ask the delivering God of the Israelites to reveal his power and set you free as you speak his truth to the church.

1. Clinging to God When Things Seem Hopeless

As we begin Exodus, the Israelites seem to be in an impossible situation. They are strangers in a strange land. They are oppressed. They are powerless. Humanly speaking, there is no way out. Yet God calls them to cling to him, even if their eyes see no hope of relief. In the same way, we need to hold fast to our God when the waters rise around us. No matter how bad the storm and no matter how great the enemy, our hope is in God.

INTERPRETIVE INSIGHT | Be Fruitful and Multiply

SIGNIFICANT SCRIPTURE

Exodus 1:1–14

At the beginning of Exodus we hear a phrase that is becoming a refrain throughout the Pentateuch. We see a theme that is close to the heart of God. It is captured in these words, "Now Joseph and all his brothers and all that generation died, but the Israelites were fruitful and multiplied greatly and became exceedingly numerous, so that the land filled with them." You might remember that in the very first command in the law, Genesis 1:28, God says, "Be fruitful and increase in number." After the Flood God repeated these words to Noah and his family, "Be fruitful and increase in number" (Genesis 9:1).

Similarly, God came to Abraham and made a promise: "I will make you fruitful; I will make nations of you" (Genesis 17:6). Abraham actually laughed because he did not think it was likely that he would be fruitful. He and Sarah had reached an age where they didn't even buy green bananas anymore. They did not think it was too likely. But they did finally receive the promised son, and now his descendants have ended up in Egypt. Nevertheless, even while they are in this furnace of oppression, they are fruitful and multiply greatly.

Who is at work here? It's God. The Israelites may not recognize it, but we can see it as we read the Bible and look back on what happened. It is no accident that the Israelites are proliferating like this. In the covenant, God promised Abraham that he would have more descendants than stars in the sky. This promise is coming true, even if the people of Israel do not recognize it.

HISTORICAL CONTEXT | Hopeless?

God had promised Abraham that his descendants would be like the sand of the seashore and the stars of the heavens and that they would populate the land of Canaan. Yet as the book of Exodus opens, this great promise seems to be in jeopardy. Abraham, Isaac, Jacob, and Joseph are dead. Their descendants are oppressed slaves in a foreign land. The idea of a great nation living in the Promised Land must have seemed like a distant dream. To the human eye, it seemed as if hope was gone.

HISTORICAL CONTEXT | Location, Location, Location!

Every real estate agent will tell you about the importance of location when it comes to buying a house. The three most important things are location, location, and location. This might be true with houses, but it is also true when it comes to the land occupied by a nation. Israel learned, very early on in their history, that the location of this Promised Land they were to occupy was critical in the world at that time (and in many ways, today as well).

In this part of the world there was something called the Fertile Crescent. This was an area that got enough rain and had enough water to sustain life. At that time in history, in that part of the world, it was all about water. Water is what made life possible, and it was crucial to travel and survival. The Fertile Crescent was one of the few places where water was available.

The Fertile Crescent started down at the Persian Gulf, crossed through the Tigris and the Euphrates Rivers, and then ran down the Mediterranean to the Nile. This is where land was habitable, crops could be grown, and people could survive. That's why it's called the *Fertile* Crescent—because things could be grown. This part of the world is known as the cradle of civilization.

All of the powers of the ancient world lived in the Fertile Crescent. The problem is that they tended to live in the north and south, and the Promised Land was right in the middle. This middle part of the Fertile Crescent became a highway for armies and trade. It was virtually impossible to go down to Egypt or up to Assyria without going through Canaan.

As the various superpowers wrestled with each other for dominance of the world, the little strip of land called Canaan (later on it was called Palestine)

CREATIVE MESSAGE IDEA | Map Time

In an effort to help your listeners grow in their understanding of the landscape where this story takes place, have them take out a piece of paper and draw a basic map with you. You can do this on a flip chart, a dry-erase board, or use the Power Point map that is provided. You can describe it your own way or use the brief description provided. The Power Point slide for this map follows what is written below.

On the left side of your paper, draw three sides of a rectangle (open at the left)—this is the Mediterranean Sea. Then down below the rectangle draw a "Y" that extends on down; this is the Nile River. Then draw what looks kind of like an arm with a hand

that's making a victory sign. This is the Red Sea. Then toward the right side here draw a little circle and a line coming down and a little oval. That's the Sea of Galilee, the Jordan River, and the Dead Sea. Finally, all the way to the right draw a kind of amoeba shape (that's the Persian Gulf) with an antenna coming up out of the amoeba that forks off into two branches. Those are the Tigris and Euphrates Rivers. The land between the Jordan and the Mediterranean Sea is the Promised Land—that's Canaan. This is the place the people of Israel want to be. With this map you can point out Egypt, the Promised Land, and the desert.

became crucial for military superiority. If Assyria or Babylonia wanted to dominate the world, they had to go through the Promised Land to get to Egypt. And if Egypt wanted to be a superpower and dominate the world, they had to defeat the Hittites to the north. It is clear to see that their armies met right in the land God had given to the people of Israel.

Not only is the land of Canaan of military importance, but it was also a critical crossroads for trade and finances. During this era, trade began to become important in the ancient world. If caravans were going to move goods, they could not get across the Arabian Desert, for there was no water. They would never make it. They had to go right through Canaan.

It is important for us to see how strategic God was in placing his people right where he did. Financially and militarily, this little piece of land had become the center of the known world. Because this land was so strategic, whatever happened there, the stories of Israel and their God would be able to spread throughout the known world as they would from no place else. It is no coincidence that God has his people positioned here to be a blessing to all the peoples on earth.

LIFE APPLICATION | Depending on God

Once Israel was back in the Promised Land, they would have many opportunities to grow in their trust of God. Because they were surrounded by all these superpowers fighting with each other, Israel would have to live in constant dependence on God because they were a small people with a modest army surrounded by massive nations with military might.

They knew every day they would have to depend on God, because Israel was never a superpower. God's mission for them did not involve that kind of power. They were never a player in the world game like Assyria, Babylonia, or Egypt. They are very rarely mentioned in ancient texts of the Egyptians and the Babylonians. Their very existence is a kind of early example of a basic principle of the kingdom of God: that often the least are the greatest of all, and those who appear to be last will be first.

Followers of Christ today live in a similar situation. In most parts of the world, Christians do not hold the seat of power or control the government. But, like Israel, we are invited to live with utter dependence on God. Our victories don't come by our might or power, but as Zechariah says, by the Spirit of the Lord. God longs to help us identify our life situations and circumstances where we do not feel powerful and in control and to look at these as opportunities to live in a day-by-day dependence on God.

> *All I have seen teaches me to trust the Creator for all I have not seen.*
> RALPH WALDO EMERSON

LIFE APPLICATION | Facing Pharaoh

This section of the Bible helps us gain a new perspective in our lives when our circumstances get desperate and we are facing a pharaoh. When we realize that God had the power to deliver his people from the hand of the pharaohs, we have hope that he can deliver us as well, and we know that we do not have to despair. We can stay faithful. We can hang on for God to deliver.

One of the great gifts God gives us in the Bible is reminders. As we look back on these real life stories of God's faithfulness, we can know that the same God is watching over us today. We need to take time to identify the pharaohs we are facing and acknowledge that God is sovereign over them. We don't have to live in fear. We don't have to run and hide. There is no oppression, no fear, no addiction, and no brokenness that is too much for God to conquer.

2. Strength in Weakness

We live in a world where the powerful rule. Yet God has a different vision for how life should work. God turns everything on its head. God exalts humble midwives above the powerful pharaoh. God uses a stammering, runaway shepherd to lead his people to freedom. God blesses an obedient wife who stands in the gap for her husband, who refuses to hold to the covenant God established. In the days of the Old Testament, as in our day, God reveals his strength in our weakness. He still exalts the humble and humbles those who exalt themselves.

HISTORICAL CONTEXT | A New King in Town

As we begin Exodus, things are looking pretty good for the Israelites. They are being very fruitful and they are multiplying. Then in Exodus 1:8, things take a turn for the worse. We read, "Then a new king, who did not know about Joseph, came to power in Egypt." There is going to be tension in Exodus from now on. This tension will become conflict and then grow to full-blown spiritual warfare. Through the first half of Exodus, things seem to get worse and worse. This new pharaoh does not care about history and what Joseph had done for Egypt four hundred years earlier. He sees all these Israelites as a threat and begins to treat them mercilessly.

On the one hand, God makes this promise, "I'm going to give you a land." On the other hand, their circumstances keep getting more and more desperate. The chances of the promise ever being fulfilled become more and more remote. The reason the writer lets us know about this tension is so that when the people of Israel are finally delivered, there will be no question that God gets the credit.

INTERPRETIVE INSIGHT | The Upside-Down Kingdom

In Exodus 1:15–17 we read, "The king of Egypt said to the Hebrew midwives, whose names were Shiphrah and Puah, 'When you help the Hebrew women in childbirth and observe them on the delivery stool, if it is a boy, kill him; but if it is a girl, let her live.' The midwives, however, feared God and did not do what the king of Egypt had told them to do; they let the boys live." These are remarkable women, and it is important that we remember their names. These two women defy a pharaoh and risk their lives in an act of heroism. They will not kill the Israelite boys. The pharaoh calls them in and asks them, "Why do you do this? Why do you let the boys live?" The women do not respond, "It's because we fear God." Rather, they say, "Well, these Hebrew women are vigorous, and their babies pop out before we can get there."

It might be helpful to pause here and address the issue of lying. This passage is not an affirmation of lying. If people ask, "Does this passage affirm lying?" you might want to say, as a short answer, "If you are ever coerced into committing mass murder by a genocidal maniac and the only way you can find to get out of this horrendous act is to deceive the genocidal maniac with a lie, I think God will understand. If, however, you try to use this passage to justify the kind of self-serving deceit that most of us engage in, which breaks community and destroys trust, that's a big mistake. This is not what God is trying to teach us in this passage."

It is interesting to note that the author of Exodus never mentions the pharaoh's name. The text never says which pharaoh Moses faces. In the hierarchy of Egypt, the pharaoh is at the top of the organizational chart and the midwives are at the very bottom. Midwives are the servants to the slaves. They don't count. But in God's organizational chart, the midwives are heroes. They risk their lives to accomplish God's purposes.

Even Abraham didn't do that. He was willing to sacrifice Sarah's well-being just to save his own scalp. Not these two brave women. It is as if God is saying, "These two women, who are nobodies in the eyes of the world, are the ones who go in my book." The first will be last. The humble will be exalted. This is the way God works.

SIGNIFICANT SCRIPTURE

Exodus 1:15–7:7

Gratitude is born in hearts that take time to count up past mercies.

CHARLES E. JEFFERSON

LIFE APPLICATION | ## Who Is Great in God's Eyes?

Sometimes we can feel unimportant, like Shiphrah and Puah. We feel as if we don't matter and nobody notices us. When this happens, God wants us to remember these two courageous women. Faithfulness really does matter! God does care about those whom the world looks right past. God is far more concerned about the condition of our hearts than the balance in our savings account or our appearance in the eyes of others. We need to live in the reality that greatness in the eyes of God is radically different from greatness in the eyes of the world.

Every time we read the names Shiphrah and Puah, we should come back to this basic truth. Over three millennia after they lived, the names of Shiphrah and Puah are still known and celebrated. Pharaoh's name didn't even make it in the book.

NARRATIVE ON THE TEXT | ## Meeting Moses

Think about what a precious gift a baby is to a mother and father. Then try to picture the Egyptians throwing boy baby after boy baby into the Nile River. There were dozens, hundreds, perhaps thousands of Hebrew babies being thrown to their death just because Pharaoh spoke the word. You look at the Nile and see the bodies of countless dead babies floating away. The people of Israel would have seen this day after day. It was becoming normative in the land of Egypt.

Out of this unthinkable genocide one baby boy is saved. His mother places him in a little waterproof basket, a custom baby boat, and sets him floating in the reeds of the Nile River. His sister watches from a distance to see what will happen to her baby brother. Will an Egyptian find him and toss him into the river like the rest of the babies?

In an ironic twist, Pharaoh's daughter finds the baby and keeps him as her own. She needs someone to nurse him, and Moses' sister Miriam offers to get a Hebrew woman. Well, guess what? She gets her mother, and baby Moses is placed back into his own home and in the arms of his own mother. On top of that, Pharaoh picks up the bill for child care. Pharaoh's daughter actually pays Moses' mother to raise her own son and places a protective wall around Moses and his family. No one is going to mess with the adopted grandson of the pharaoh.

As Moses grows, he finds himself living in two worlds. He's concerned for his people, the Hebrews, but he is educated and trained as an Egyptian. In Exodus 2:11–12 we read, "One day, after Moses had grown up, he went out to where his own people were and watched them at their hard labor. He saw an Egyptian beating a Hebrew, one of his own people. Glancing this way and that and seeing no one, he killed the Egyptian and hid him in the sand." Moses had the freedom of an Egyptian, but his heart was still with his own people.

LIFE APPLICATION | Looking This Way and That

We read that Moses looks "this way and that." He looks to the right and looks to the left. Which way does he not look? He does not look up. He does not think about God. Moses looks around him to be sure he will not be caught in his act of murdering an Egyptian. When he sees that the coast is clear, he acts on his human impulse to vindicate his people. But Moses does not stop to look up to his God and seek heavenly counsel or wisdom.

We can easily repeat Moses' error. We might not look "this way and that" and then kill someone, but we can be just as guilty of forgetting to look up to God in moments of need. It is the husband who is out of town on business and meets an attractive woman in his travels. He looks this way and that and is certain no one will ever know. He tells himself that what his wife does not know won't hurt her. The coast is clear, but he forgets to look up to God and realize that God sees and cares deeply about the decisions he is about to make. It is the college student who looks this way and that and then decides to cheat, just a little, on her exams, because no one will ever know. It is the businessman who knows the deal is shady, but he can cover his tracks and everyone else is doing it.

Just as Moses was tempted to look around and be sure no one was looking before he acted on his sinful impulses, so we can be tempted to do the same. We need to learn to look upward, into the eyes of the God who sees and cares.

PAUSE FOR PRAYER

A Time for Thanksgiving

Just as pharaohs still live, so do Shiphras and Puahs. We have all met wonderful people who follow Christ with a deep humility, the heart of a servant, and a passion to faithfully follow the Savior. Take time to offer prayers of thanksgiving for the Shiphrahs and Puahs in the lives of those gathered. In your church it might be most appropriate to do this silently. If it is normative or appropriate to do this out loud, consider doing this as well.

NARRATIVE ON THE TEXT | ## Moses in Midian

Even though Moses looks "this way and that" before he strikes out against the Egyptian, he still gets caught. What a vivid reminder that no matter how hard we look before we sin or try to cover our tracks after we have acted on sinful impulses, it seems someone always finds out. This is true for Moses—and it is true in most of our lives as well. Word of what Moses did hits the street like front-page news, and Pharaoh gets word of it in no time at all. To make things worse, Pharaoh puts a price on his head. So Moses runs for his life and ends up in the land of the Midianites.

When Moses gets to Midian, he is sitting by a well and notices some young women with flocks who are being chased from a well by a group of surly shepherds. Apparently Moses has a passion for justice and cannot stand to see people oppressed, because here he single-handedly comes to the rescue of these women. He ends up marrying one of them, a woman named Zipporah. He has a son, and it looks as if he will spend the rest of his life as a shepherd far away from his own people in Egypt. But there is some backstage action going on in heaven. God is at work, and Moses is about to enter a whole new chapter of his life.

Exodus 2:23–25 says, "During that long period, the king of Egypt died. The Israelites groaned in their slavery and cried out, and their cry for help because of their slavery went up to God. God heard their groaning and he remembered his covenant with Abraham, with Isaac and with Jacob. So God looked on the Israelites and was concerned about them." Moses is busy tending sheep and raising a family, very ordinary things. God is busy preparing a leader to bring his people out of Egypt, something extraordinary. What Moses does not yet know is that he will be this leader.

WORD STUDY
Remembered

In Exodus 2:24 we read, "God heard their groaning and he remembered his covenant with Abraham, with Isaac and with Jacob." When the Bible says "God remembered," it doesn't mean he had forgotten. Anytime you see the expression "God remembered" in the Old Testament, it means God is about to act. Watch out, God is going to do something. When you read about God's remembering something, don't get the idea that he has a short memory; rather, be encouraged that God takes action on behalf of his people.

INTERPRETIVE INSIGHT | ## Turning Aside

Moses was leading a fairly ordinary and uneventful life in Midian. Some might have called it boring. For about forty years he took care of sheep. But one day, everything changes. In Exodus 3:1–3 we read:

> Now Moses was tending the flock of Jethro his father-in-law,
> the priest of Midian, and he led the flock to the far side of the
> desert and came to Horeb, the mountain of God. There the angel
> of the LORD appeared to him in flames of fire from within a bush.
> Moses saw that though the bush was on fire it did not burn up.
> So Moses thought, "I will go over and see this strange sight—
> why the bush does not burn up."

Once again, God shows up in the most unexpected place. When this happens, Moses makes a decision that will change his life. The New Revised Standard Version translation of verse 3 is, "Moses says, 'I must *turn aside* and look at this great sight, and see why the bush does not burn up.'" There is a sense in which everything hinges on Moses' decision to turn aside. He doesn't have to do that. He could have said, "I'm a busy man with much to do. I don't have time to turn aside." He just would have missed his calling. He would have missed the Exodus. He would have missed the reason for which he was born.

LIFE APPLICATION | Being Willing to Stop and Listen

Pause for a moment and invite your listeners to look at their lives and ask themselves how they are doing at *turning aside*. Remind them of the things you talked about last week at the end of the message about going on a God hunt. How are they doing? Are they slowing down and noticing God more? Are there burning bushes they need to turn aside and look at? Are there places where God was present, where they've stopped, and where they've met him? Did they hear promptings and follow them? Are there answered prayers they should celebrate?

INTERPRETIVE INSIGHT | The Heart of God

Moses did what many of us miss. He turned aside and met with God. In Exodus 3:5 God says to him, "Do not come any closer. Take off your sandals, for the place where you are standing is holy ground." That's the first occurrence of the word "holy" in Scripture.

Then we read in verses 7–8:

> The LORD said, "I have indeed seen the misery of my people.
> I have heard them crying out because of their slave drivers, and I
> am concerned about their suffering. So I have come down to
> rescue them from the hand of the Egyptians and to bring them
> up out of that land into a good and spacious land, a land flowing
> with milk and honey."

The heart of God cries out from the far reaches of history and the pages of Scripture. "I love my people! I long for their good. I want to deliver them." God says, "I have seen, I have noticed, I care, I've come down, I want to bring my salvation."

What a God we serve! He loves us as children and wants to lead and guide us. He hears our prayers when we cry to him. He loves to pour out his goodness on his people.

INTERPRETIVE INSIGHT | Five Objections

At this point, Moses launches into a series of five objections. He is much like the rest of us. He believes in God's power, but he is not so sure about himself. He does not feel up to the task and worthy of the calling.

Moses' first objection is, "Who am I?" It is an argument from a feeling of inadequacy. God simply responds by saying, "I will be with you." God wants Moses to understand that his own pedigree or power are not the issue, only God's presence.

Next, Moses asks, "Who are you?" This is an argument of authority. Moses knows he will have to tell others about this God and he needs to know whom he is dealing with. God's response is short and to the point, "I AM WHO I AM." God reveals the great name Yahweh and tells Moses that he is the eternal God who always is.

Moses then presents his third objection: What will he do if the people will not listen to him? Moses is afraid the people will think he has made the whole thing up. His own authority and integrity may be questioned. Again, God is patient. He asks Moses a question, "What is that in your hand?" By now we know that when God starts asking questions, things get interesting. Moses says, "It's a staff." God says, "Throw it on the ground." Moses does so, and the text tells us that it becomes a snake and Moses runs away from it.

ON THE LIGHTER SIDE | I've Got a Job for You

There's all this good news: "I've noticed, I've come down. So now, Moses, you go to Pharaoh, the tyrannical dictator of the most powerful nation on earth, who may still have a bounty on your head, and tell him to let his prime labor force go for no reason at all. Remember to check in with me when you're finished. Then I may have a difficult job for you this afternoon."

It is quite humorous when you read the passage. God tells Moses that he has been watching his chosen people and he is very aware of their plight. God has seen, he has heard, he is concerned, and he will rescue them. But then he adds, almost as an afterthought, "and by the way Moses, you will be the one to accomplish my purposes and deliver the people." Can you imagine the look on Moses' face?

Notice a little detail that is often missed. In Exodus 4:4 we read: "Then the LORD said to him, 'Reach out your hand and take it by the tail.'" In the unlikely event that you were going to pick up a dangerous snake, where do you think you'd pick it up? Right behind the head. Definitely not the tail—that's the most vulnerable thing to do. But God is saying, "Moses, trust me. You're going to have to get used to dealing with snakes and other sorts of dangers, so you might as well start now. Go for the tail." God gives Moses a few other miracles, but Moses is still not ready to sign on.

In Exodus 4:10, Moses offers a fourth objection. In effect he says, "Speaking is not one of my core competencies." Moses tells God that he does not feel his public speaking skills are sharp enough for this particular task. But God counters by telling Moses, "Not a problem. I'm in charge of spiritual gifts. I can take care of that. I made your mouth and I can give you all you need to speak to Pharaoh."

Finally Moses is out of formal excuses, so he unloads his fifth and final effort to get out of this calling. He swallows hard and gives God a little advice: "God, please send someone else." God gets stern with Moses at this point and makes Moses an offer he cannot refuse. "You go, and I will send Aaron with you as a partner. He can be your spokesman." Grudgingly Moses says, "All right, I'll do it."

WORD STUDY

Yahweh

The name Yahweh is used almost seven thousand times in the Old Testament. It was so revered by the Jewish people that they wouldn't even pronounce it. We don't even know the exact, correct pronunciation because they wouldn't say it out loud out of reverence.

Its significance here means that God is saying, "I'll make myself known to you." That's what telling someone your name was all about in Bible times. It is as if God is saying, "I'll reveal my character, my identity. I am the God who knows and sees and cares and acts. I am with you."

HISTORICAL CONTEXT | Blood Kin

Before Moses goes to Pharaoh, there is a unique episode recorded in Exodus 4:24–26. This account of Zipporah circumcising her son, touching Moses' feet with the foreskin, and then calling Moses a "bridegroom of blood" seems very odd. On top of that, we read that God was about to kill Moses and the actions of his quick-thinking wife saved his life. This also seems out of place.

There is a fair amount of consensus among Old Testament scholars that this is a story about the profound importance of circumcision in the covenant. Circumcision was a kind of signature on the part of a person, which meant they wanted to be in a covenant relationship with God. Apparently Moses had not

circumcised his son, although he knew he should have. Most likely, he has not been circumcised himself, which means he is deliberately disobeying God. He is holding himself outside of a covenant relationship with the Lord. There is simply no way he can take on God's mission until this is remedied.

So Zipporah, his wife, recognizing what's happening, takes a flint knife—the appropriate instrument—and circumcises their son. Then she touches Moses' feet. The word for feet is often a euphemism in Semitic culture for genitals. She touches him as a kind of temporary, vicarious circumcision of Moses until the time comes when Moses can be properly circumcised.

When Zipporah makes that statement about "you're a bridegroom of blood to me," it might sound like a negative thing to say, like, "What a lot of bloodshed you and your God are causing me." But this is not what she is saying. It was actually a ritual marriage statement that a Hebrew bride would make when her groom had been circumcised before marriage. It's a positive statement: "You are blood kin to me. We're members of one family. We're a covenant people together." What's really happening here is that Moses has been disobedient to God's covenant calling. God is serious about it, and Zipporah's quick insight and actions save the day.

NARRATIVE ON LIFE | Heroes in the Pentateuch

Here is a short note about heroes in the beginning of Exodus. Here is a list of the heroes:

- the two midwives, who save the Israelites
- Moses' mom, who risks her life to save her son
- Moses' sister, who stands guard over him
- Pharaoh's daughter, who defies her father to raise Moses
- Moses' wife, who corrects his disobedience

Notice the one trait these all have in common? They're all women! It is a striking reality that in a highly patriarchal world, God keeps using women to accomplish his purposes.

NARRATIVE ON THE TEXT | Facing Pharaoh

Moses goes to the people of Israel, tells them what God says, and shows them the signs God gave him, and they seem to be on board with the whole plan. They accept his words and bow down and worship God. Everything is working according to plan. The last detail is to get Pharaoh's signoff, and then Moses and the people of Israel are home free. So Moses goes to Pharaoh and says, "This is what the LORD, the God of Israel, says: 'Let my people go, so that they may hold a festival to me in the desert'" (Exodus 5:1).

This is a bold way to approach the most powerful man in the world. There is no small talk or preparation. Moses stands and makes God's plan clear. The people of Israel want to pack up and head out into the desert to meet with their God.

But Pharaoh is not ready to see his slave labor take a vacation. So he responds, "Why are you taking these people away from their labor? Get back to work!" (Exodus 5:4). Pharaoh's take on this whole deal is clear: "They are lazy; that's why they are crying out, 'Let us go and sacrifice to our God.' So make them work harder. That way they will keep working and pay no attention to lies."

ON THE LIGHTER SIDE | Servant Leadership

As we look at Pharaoh, we discover that he is not into servant leadership. He is not a team-empowering, people-building kind of guy. He is not into the inverted pyramids where the top guy is on the bottom and serves others. He is into the original pyramids, where the top guy is on the top. Because he built the original pyramids, he thinks that's a good way to structure things.

From a human perspective, it seems as if the whole thing has backfired and exploded in Moses' face.

NARRATIVE ON THE TEXT | A Word of Hope

Pharaoh asks, "Who is this Yahweh? I am not impressed." Moses looks at how things are proceeding and struggles because this is not what he has signed up for. The Israelites think, "We might as well go to Pharaoh. We're already slaves. It can't get any worse." And then guess what happens? It gets worse. So they complain. "We don't want to make bricks without straw. What have you done to us?" they say to Moses. "You have made us stink to Pharaoh." The people of Israel are not happy with Moses at this point and blame him for how badly things are going.

Moses is left alone—just he and Aaron. But now he is not only pitted against Pharaoh in Egypt, but the people of Israel are angry with him as well. In the midst this turmoil and fear, God offers reassurance. He says in Exodus 6:6–7:

> "Therefore, say to the Israelites: 'I am the LORD, and I will bring you out from the under the yoke of the Egyptians. I will free you from being slaves to them, and I will redeem you with an outstretched arm and with mighty acts of judgment. I will take you as my own people, and I will be your God. Then you will know that I am the LORD your God.'"

Even in times of conflict, pain, and struggle, God speaks a word of hope.

LIFE APPLICATION | Facing Discouragement

Exodus 6:9 reveals a deep heart problem in the people of Israel. It is a poignant verse, "Moses reported this to the Israelites, but they did not listen to him because of their discouragement and cruel bondage." Discouragement will crush a human spirit. The people of God are deaf to good news from God because they are discouraged. There are times when each one of us needs to be reminded that a discouraged spirit keeps us from hearing and following God's voice. God wants to say to us, "Don't let discouragement have the last word. I am still at work, and I who delivered my people a long time ago, I can deliver you. Keep looking for me. Keep trusting me. Keep waiting. Keep obeying."

Challenge your listeners to resist giving in to discouragement. Remind them that they will face many hard situations in life, but with God in the equation, there is always hope. Invite people to identify where they feel discouraged and to seek God to lift the dark cloud of discouragement and to pray for his light to shine through.

PAUSE FOR PRAYER

An Attitude Check

Some people see the cup half full; others see it half empty. There is yet another group of people who see the cup full and overflowing, even if it "looks" half full. Pause for a time of silent listening prayer. Call the people gathered to inspect their hearts. Does a spirit of discouragement rule them? Do they have a negative attitude that hangs over them like a dark cloud? Or do they have a healthy and godly optimism? Do they see the presence of God, even in hard times?

Pray for each person to come to a place of freedom from discouragement. Pray also that they will be released as bearers of God's encouragement and blessing in the lives of those they encounter each day.

SIGNIFICANT SCRIPTURE

Exodus 7:8–12:42

Also challenge those who are feeling strong and encouraged to be a blessing to others around them. If they know someone who is going through the valley of discouragement, challenge them to take a role as an encourager. Challenge them to pray, love, and bless those who are hurting. In this way, they can be used as a messenger of God's encouragement.

3. The God Who Delivers

Little children love to say, "I can do it myself!" Often, this makes their parents proud. But when it comes to deliverance, God does not want to hear these words from the mouths of his children. We can't do it on our own. The Israelites couldn't, and neither can we. We need God's heavenly power and mighty help. Like the people of Israel, we need to come to a point where we cry out to the one who loves to bring deliverance to his children.

NARRATIVE ON THE TEXT | ## The Plagues Begin

Now the battle starts. God initiates a series of "plagues" or "mighty acts" on Pharaoh and Egypt. In the first one, the Nile River is turned to blood. This would have deep meaning for the Israelites. Remember, the Nile had been filled with the blood of their infants. It would be significant for them to see God bringing justice for the heartless brutality of the Egyptians.

The second plague has quite a different tone to it. God sends frogs, and the writer deliberately paints a picture to ridicule the pretensions of Pharaoh. Notice the detail he gives in Exodus 8:1–4:

> "This is what the LORD says: 'Let my people go so that they can worship me. If you refuse to let them go, I will plague your whole country with frogs. The Nile will teem with frogs. They will come up into your palace and your bedroom and onto your bed, into the houses of your officials and on your people, and into your ovens and kneading troughs. The frogs will go up on you and your people and all your officials.'"

The writer is specific about how bad this plague of frogs will be.

INTERPRETIVE INSIGHT | The Signs of a Hard Heart

There's a pattern developing with Pharaoh. It starts with a hard-hitting plague, followed by what looks like repentance, then next comes the plea for deliverance, and finally Pharaoh's heart becomes hard again. Plague after plague continues: gnats, flies, dying livestock, boils, hail, locusts, and darkness all come to Egypt. Again and again Pharaoh seems to repent but later ends up with a hard heart.

In Exodus 9:27–28 we see an interesting dynamic of the way sin works. After the plague of the hail Pharaoh calls Moses and confesses. "'This time I have sinned,' he said to them. 'The Lord is in the right, and I and my people are in the wrong. Pray to the Lord, for we have had enough thunder and hail. I will let you go; you don't have to stay any longer.'"

Every outward indication would give the impression that he is repenting. He even says, "I have sinned." In verse 34 Moses prays, and God stops the plague of hail. Then we read, "When Pharaoh saw that the rain and hail and thunder had stopped, he sinned again: He and his officials hardened their hearts."

When the pain is intense, Pharaoh says, "I have sinned. I will change." When the pain goes away, his repentance goes away too. He never really repents. He is just trying to avoid the pain he is feeling.

This can happen with people who seek to follow Christ. When they are in intense pain, their spiritual sensitivity seems to go up. But when the pain goes away, so does their openness to God. Their willingness to surrender is contingent on the presence of pain. Their willingness to submit and obey evaporates like the morning dew after the pain is over.

ON THE LIGHTER SIDE | Frogs and Pharaoh

Do you get the picture? Frogs in your house, frogs in the bedroom, frogs in the bed, frogs everywhere. The frogs are getting real disruptive of daily life. It's hard to get a good night of sleep when the bed is full of frogs. On top of this, there are frogs in the kitchen. There are going to be frogs in the microwave, in the mixing bowls, frogs in the pizza, and frogs on the cereal. The people of Egypt had better get used to the taste of frogs! There will be frogs in the garage getting crunched under the wheels of the royal chariot.

Now, here is where things get humorous. Guess what Pharaoh's magicians do to show their great power? *They make more frogs.* By this time, Pharaoh must be getting a little tired of frogs. He actually says to Moses, "Pray to the Lord to take the frogs away from me and my people" (Exodus 8:8).

An author/comedian named Ken Davis sees great humor in Pharaoh's response. You see, Moses tells Pharaoh to name the time he is ready to be rid of the frogs. When Pharaoh gives a time, Moses will pray and the frogs will be done with. Now, guess what Pharaoh says? "How about tomorrow?" It is as if Pharaoh is saying, "Let me have one more night with the frogs in the bed, one more meal with frogs in my bowl, and one more drive with frogs all over the roads." How strange is that?

LIFE APPLICATION True Repentance or Pain Control?

Pharaoh is never really repentant; he is just trying to do pain control. We can do the same thing. We must learn to ask ourselves a simple question: Am I really repenting right now or am I just trying to do pain control with God? If we see that our repentance is just a way to get quick relief but we have no intention of changing our behavior or attitudes, we are not truly repentant.

Take time for those gathered to reflect on their patterns of repentance. If they are responding only in an effort to avoid personal pain, invite them to look to the heart of God. Seeing God's pain over our sin leads to repentance.

NARRATIVE ON THE TEXT The Passover

The tenth and final plague is the most devastating of all. God sends the angel of death and takes the firstborn in the Egyptian households. The people who committed genocide against the Israelites now lose their firstborn.

Imagine for a moment being in one of the Israelite homes on that night. God tells his people, "This is what the LORD says: 'About midnight I will go throughout Egypt. Every firstborn son in Egypt will die, from the firstborn son of Pharaoh, who sits on the throne, to the firstborn son of the slave girl, who is at her hand mill'" (Exodus 11:4–5). Imagine being in the home of one of the Israelites on that night. God has told you to get ready to leave. God has told you, "Sacrifice a lamb and put the blood of the lamb on the door frames around your home, and I will pass over your home. Death and judgment will pass over you and your family because you're covered by the blood of the lamb." So, in obedience, you slaughter a lamb, put the blood on your doorpost, and wait. It must have been the most awful night of darkness, death, and judgment in history.

You wonder if this is real. Will the angel of death come? Will your children be spared? Will judgment be poured out on the Egyptians? You are hardly able to breathe all night long. But God is true to his word. He passes over all the houses of Israel, which are covered by the blood of the lamb. This picture of the Passover, the deliverance from death, prefigures the salvation that will belong to all of God's people who are covered with the blood of Jesus Christ, the Lamb of God.

LIFE APPLICATION | Lord, Deliver Me!

As you close this message, you might want to ask a personal question of those gathered: *Is there anywhere in your life where you need God the deliverer?*

Invite the people to close their eyes for a moment and talk with God about this. *Is there any sin or temptation that feels like it has got a hold on you? Has hardness of heart taken hold of you as it took hold of Pharaoh? Maybe it is a pattern of sin. It might be a habit that has been there for a long time.*

Invite people to ask God for deliverance and then to do whatever God tells them to do to walk toward freedom.

You might want to give other simple promptings to help people reflect on areas in which they might need deliverance, such as:

> *Maybe you're in a real difficult situation or a troubling relationship.*
>
> *Maybe you've made a commitment to God in some area of your life, and it's getting hard.*
>
> *Maybe you feel trapped in a financial commitment and now things are difficult.*
>
> *Maybe you made a commitment to read through the Old Testament, and it's just getting hard.*
>
> *Maybe, like the Israelites, you're just beaten down and discouraged.*

After a time of silent reflection, pray for each person to find the deliverance they need in the saving power of the God who set Israel free from Egypt.

God the Lawgiver

Brief Message
OUTLINE

1 Understanding the Holiness of God

2 Are People Saved by Obeying Laws We Read in the Old Testament?

3 Why Is There So Much Detail in These Laws?

4 How Do We Know What Laws We Are to Obey Today?

The Heart of the
MESSAGE

God is perfectly holy. We are not. We are an unholy people desperately seeking a way to grow in holiness! How do impure people learn to walk in holiness?

The answer is: We walk with a God who is holy, and he transforms us. First, he *makes us holy* through his cleansing power and grace. Second, he teaches us to *grow in holiness* as we learn to walk in his ways. The people of Israel learned that growing in holiness is a process that takes a lifetime. As a nation, they learned that the journey toward holiness carries over many generations and centuries.

As we study the book of Leviticus (and other books of the Pentateuch), we discover that God makes us holy as we enter into a living relationship with him through Jesus Christ. Yet, holiness is also something that continues growing in us for a lifetime. In this message we will hear the invitation of God to grow in holiness. We will be called to transformed lives as we hear the living God say:

> I am the LORD your God; consecrate yourselves and be holy, because I am holy. Do not make yourselves unclean by any creature that moves about on the ground. I am the LORD who brought you up out of Egypt to be your God; therefore be holy, because I am holy. (Leviticus 11:44–45)

The Heart of the
MESSENGER

The truth revealed in Leviticus peels back the facade of self-righteousness and reveals the true condition of our hearts and lives. We are impure and tainted by sin. The message of Leviticus is both painful and freeing. It is painful because it shows us the depth of our sin. It is freeing because it reveals a God of holiness who has the power to make us more like him than we ever dreamed.

Take time as you prepare to teach this message and meditate on the first half of Leviticus 11:44, "I am the LORD your God; consecrate yourselves and be holy, because I am holy." Ask the Holy Spirit to shine the light of holiness on your life and reveal any areas you need to consecrate to the Lord. Begin praying for holiness to grow in your life.

1. Understanding the Holiness of God

All things being equal, we prefer purity. If we can have coffee made from beans that are only 9 percent infested with insects, or coffee that is 100 percent free of insects, we prefer the pure stuff. When it comes to our food and beverages, we are all in favor of purity.

But when it comes to our own lives, we give ourselves a fair amount of latitude. "After all, we're only human," we say as we justify our impurity. We're prepared to put up with a lower standard when it comes to us. The FDA tells us what is pure enough when it comes to our food. We try to do the same with our lives. The problem is that we work on a sliding scale. Our idea of purity is a far cry from God's definition. God is holy, and he is committed to seeing us grow in holiness.

NARRATIVE ON THE TEXT | Impure People Called to Holiness

SIGNIFICANT SCRIPTURE

Exodus 19

In Exodus 19 we come to the foot of Mount Sinai. Here we see a ragtag group of frightened, grumbling, fugitive slaves. They have no real sense of identity yet, and no clear knowledge of God. They are thoroughly impure. They are ready to run back to Egypt at the first sign of difficulty.

What is amazing is that God is banking his whole hope to redeem the world on these people. How can God possibly get them to appreciate how high the stakes are? What must he do to help them see that their little lives matter so much? God longs to help these people understand that there is another way to live besides the kind of grasping, clutching, grubbing, and grabbing they have grown accustomed to.

ON THE LIGHTER SIDE | What Is Purity?

Our society has certain standards and laws designed to guard purity. A whole department of our federal government, the Food and Drug Administration, functions as a watchdog for purity. However, their standards of what counts as pure are surprising.

The standards below come directly from the Food and Drug Administration:

Apple butter: If apple butter averages four or more rodent hairs per 100 grams, or if it averages five or more whole insects, not counting mites or aphids (which are OK with the U.S. government), the FDA will pull it from the shelves. Otherwise, it goes right on your bagel.

Mushrooms: When you get 15 grams of mushrooms, they're OK unless they contain an average of 20 or more maggots of any size.

Fig paste: If there are more than 13 insect heads per 100 grams, the FDA will toss it out. Apparently other insect body parts are OK, but we don't want to have to look at their little insect faces.

Coffee beans: All the caffeine addicts can get a little nervous now. Coffee beans are only withdrawn from the market if an average of 10 percent or more of them are insect infested.

Hotdogs: You don't even want to know. If they took all the impurities out of a hot dog, there would be nothing left.

In an effort to help the people see the magnitude of his plan, God speaks to Moses in Exodus 19:3–6:

> "This is what you are to say to the house of Jacob and what you are to tell the people of Israel: 'You yourselves have seen what I did to Egypt, and how I carried you on eagles' wings and brought you to myself. Now if you obey me fully and keep my covenant, then out of all nations you will be my treasured possession. Although the whole earth is mine, you will be for me a kingdom of priests and a holy nation.' These are the words you are to speak to the Israelites."

You can almost see this fearful group of wanderers standing in stunned amazement as they begin to realize that God is serious! His plan to impact and reach the whole world with his love will be built on this group of people. And to accomplish this great purpose, this people will need to grow in holiness.

LIFE APPLICATION | Purity of Heart

The standard for hotdogs, fig paste, and even coffee is not nearly as pure as we think it should be. This is also true of our hearts. It's true of our words. It's true of our minds. It's true of our culture, media, and relationships. We live in an impure world.

Every human being alive convinces himself or herself that, "My little impurities don't really matter. They don't really amount to much. They're really quite tolerable." But add them all up, and you have the tragedy of the world in which we live, the downward spiral of human sin.

Every follower of Christ needs to do a regular heart inventory and see where impurity is creeping in. We need to ask the Holy Spirit to search our hearts and reveal where we need to grow in purity and be purged of impurity (see Psalm 139:23–24).

INTERPRETIVE INSIGHT | The Love of God

Before God ever gives the Ten Commandments, he reminds Israel of his loving concern for them: "I carried you on eagles' wings" (Exodus 19:4). God describes his intention and vision for their future with three phrases that they will never forget (Exodus 19:5–6).

He says, *"You'll be a treasured possession."* This little, insignificant, wanna-be nation really matters to God. He also declares, *"You'll be a kingdom of priests."*

A true and faithful Christian does not make holy living a mere incidental thing. It is his great concern. As the business of the soldier is to fight, so the business of the Christian is to be like Christ.

JONATHAN EDWARDS

PAUSE FOR PRAYER

Search Me, O God!

Allow a time for silent prayer. Invite people to listen for the Holy Spirit to begin speaking to them about areas of impurity that need to be cleansed and areas they need to grow in purity. After a time of silent listening, lead in a prayer for each person to grow in purity.

Every person can relate directly to God. They will have access to God and be in a relationship with their Creator. Finally, he says, *"You'll be a holy nation."* God lets them know that they will be a model community set apart to draw all the peoples of the earth to God.

INTERPRETIVE INSIGHT | Preparing to Meet God

The people go to great extents as they prepare to meet with God. In Exodus 19:10–11 we read, "And the LORD said to Moses, 'Go to the people and consecrate them today and tomorrow. Have them wash their clothes and be ready by the third day, because on that day the LORD will come down on Mount Sinai in the sight of all the people."

Certain limits are placed around the mountain. They are told not to touch the mountain. They are even told to abstain from sexual activity as they prepare their hearts, minds, and bodies to meet with God.

LIFE APPLICATION | Being Prepared

Too often we approach God with a casual attitude. There is a place for confidence when we draw near to God, and we know that his arms are wide open to his beloved children. But God is the mighty and holy Creator of heaven and earth. His power is beyond our wildest dreams. Like the people of Israel, we need to learn to prepare to meet with God. This is particularly true as we think about gathering together in corporate worship with the community of God's people.

There are many things we can do to prepare ourselves to gather with God's people and meet with our heavenly Father. Here are just a few ideas:

- Seek to go to worship feeling physically rested. If you go to morning services, be sure to get to bed at a reasonable time.

- If you drive to church services alone or with others, use the time to pray. Pray for the Spirit to move, pray for your heart to be soft, pray for those who will be leading worship, pray for visitors who might come, and pray for anything else that comes to your heart.

- Arrive early enough that you can park, get into the building, visit with those you meet, but still sit down five or ten minutes before the service begins. Use this time to quiet your heart, confess your sins, and tune in to God's still small voice.

WORD STUDY
Holiness

Originally, at its root, the word "holy" simply meant "set apart." This word pointed to things that were reserved for a special use and were not to be touched or used for anything else. Later the word "holy" began to point to moral purity, but at the root of the word is the idea of something (or someone) that is set apart.

In the Bible many objects are said to be holy. In Exodus 3, when Moses was on this same mountain, God said, "Take off your shoes, because this is holy ground." In this passage the mountain is said to be holy. Sometimes clothing or certain foods are declared holy in the Bible. These things are set apart.

ILLUSTRATION | Holy Cake

Here is a modern-day example, as told by John Ortberg, of something that was set apart (the meaning of "holy"). You can tell this story or one from your life that communicates a similar message.

> I got home from work on a Friday evening. My daughter had made chocolate cake with homemade frosting. Personally, I think chocolate cake is one of the greatest proofs for the existence of God in the world!
>
> Here was the dilemma: She had made this particular chocolate cake for another group of people. It was not for our family. It was not for me! So, right next to the cake there was a single piece of paper, and on that paper was one single word, "NO!" This word cried out from the paper because it was followed by several exclamation points. This note was intended for me, the father of the family. She knew it, I knew it, and everyone who read the note knew whom the cake-maker was thinking of when she wrote the note.
>
> The message was real clear and echoed with a message that went all the way back to the book of Genesis: "From every other cake in the house you may freely eat, but of this cake, the chocolate cake, you may not eat, for on the day you eat thereof, you shall surely die." This cake was set apart—holy.

INTERPRETIVE INSIGHT | The Holiness of God

The objects in the Bible that are declared holy are not holy in themselves. Only God is holy in himself, and only God can make something holy when he touches it. Objects become holy when they are set apart for God's use.

Something unique and important happened in Israel's understanding of holiness as time passed. The holiness that sets God apart came to be understood, above all else, as his moral excellence, his blinding purity, his perfect character. This God was set apart from sin.

Now, here is the problem: This holy God is in relationship with this group of people at the foot of the mountain, and they are steeped in sin. He is also in relationship with us, and we are no less tainted by sin than the people we read about in Exodus. Since the Fall, every human being who has walked this earth (except Jesus) has been marked by sin, and this leads to a terrible ambivalence toward this holy God. We are drawn to holiness, we hunger for it, but we are afraid of it. We long for it, we know we need it, and yet we fear it will destroy us.

ILLUSTRATION | Meeting Aslan

In C. S. Lewis's Narnia Chronicles, one of the characters (Lucy) hears a description of the Christ figure, Aslan. It occurs to her, for the first time, that she might be a little nervous if she were to come face to face with this magnificent being. Mrs. Beaver (one of the many talking animals in the land of Narnia) says to her, "That you will, dearie, and no mistake. If there's anyone who can appear before Aslan without their knees knocking, they're either braver than most or else just silly."

"Then he isn't safe?" asks Lucy.

Mr. Beaver answers, "Safe? Don't you hear what Mrs. Beaver tells you? Who said anything about safe? 'Course he isn't safe. But he's good. He's the king, I tell you."

CREATIVE MESSAGE IDEA | The Holiness of God

As you are teaching about the holiness of God, read Exodus 19:16 and then invite people to imagine the power, majesty, and holiness of God while they listen and watch. If you have the technical ability to do this, have a brief light show with trumpet blasts and thunderous sounds! Invite the people to imagine what it might have felt like to have been there with the people of Israel as God descended on the mountain in this earth-shattering theophany.

Read:

On the morning of the third day there was thunder and lightning, with a thick cloud over the mountain, and a very loud trumpet blast. Everyone in the camp trembled. Then Moses led the people out of the camp to meet with God, and they stood at the foot of the mountain. Mount Sinai was covered with smoke, because the LORD descended on it in fire. The smoke billowed up from it like smoke from a furnace, the whole mountain trembled violently, and the sound of the trumpet grew louder and louder. Then Moses spoke and the voice of God answered him. (Exodus 19:16–19)

After the lights stop and the room quiets, explain that the trumpet blast was associated in Israel with the sound of worship. It meant, "The Lord, Yahweh, is coming." In this passage we read of the trumpets blasting, but there's no human being blowing the trumpet. God is announcing his own arrival. Everyone trembles because they know that God is near.

You Will Need:
- The ability to create the appearance of lightning with your lights
- Someone to run the lights and be ready to give the best light show they can
- The ability to make thunderous sound and trumpet blasts. These can be live or pre-recorded. If you can create a low bass sound that will make the building shake, go for it!
- If you have the capability to safely have smoke billow from the stage down into the congregation, this would add to the effect

INTERPRETIVE INSIGHT | A Consuming Fire

There are many statements in Scripture that teach of the reality of God's holiness. In Deuteronomy 4:24 Moses says, "For the LORD your God is a consuming fire." In Exodus 20:20 we read, "Moses said to the people, 'Do not be afraid. God has come to test you, so that the fear of God will be with you to keep you from sinning.'" Notice the paradox. The people say, "Keep him at a distance from us! He's not safe." Yet at the same time, they long to draw near to God.

It is as if Moses is saying, "Who said anything about safe? He is coming to put the fear of God in you so that you will be done with the folly and destructiveness of sin. Of course he's not safe. But he's good. Don't be afraid." On this mountain God speaks. He gives the Ten Commandments, the cornerstone of ethical guidelines for his people. These teachings have changed the world.

LIFE APPLICATION | In the Light of His Holiness

Imagine for a moment what it would be like for an unholy people to come into the presence of a holy God. If you want to know the people's response to this real-life experience, look at Exodus 20:18–19: "When the people saw the thunder and lightning and heard the trumpet and saw the mountain in smoke, they trembled with fear. They stayed at a distance and said to Moses, 'Speak to us yourself and we will listen. But do not have God speak to us or we will die.'"

This is a constant theme in Scripture. When people really encounter a holy God, the first thing that happens is they are overwhelmed and undone by their own sense of sinfulness. In Isaiah 6:5 we read a magnificent vision of God in the greatness of his holiness, and we see Isaiah's response: "Woe to me! . . . I am ruined! For I am a man of unclean lips, and I live among a people of unclean lips, and my eyes have seen the King, the LORD Almighty." In the New Testament, Peter sees the reality of Jesus' power and holiness, and his response is, "Go away from me, Lord! I am a sinful man" (Luke 5:8).

Each one of us needs to come to the mountain and see God, in all his power and glory. We need to fall on our faces in the radiating light of his holiness and be overwhelmed with the reality of our sin and his purity. We need an Isaiah moment, where we cry out, "Woe is me!" These are the moments that we stop making excuses, stop rationalizing, and stop defending the indefensible.

True faith can no more be without holiness than fire without heat.

JOHN OWEN

2. Are People Saved by Obeying the Law?

Sometimes people read the Old Testament and they say something like this, "You know, I think the God of the Old Testament is all about the law. The old covenant means people got saved by keeping the law. Are you trying to tell me that the God of the Old Testament is a God of grace? No way! He is all about law."

These people, who are often well meaning, have this idea that some people attain salvation by following specific biblical rules and regulations. In this section of the message we must be very clear on this issue. The law, including the Ten Commandments, was never given to people so they could earn God's favor. That was never God's way of dealing with human problems. These laws were given to them after God had already been gracious to them and reached out to them with tender love.

HISTORICAL CONTEXT | Ancient Covenants

One of the exciting archaeological discoveries of the last century has been the unearthing of many ancient treaties (covenants) from the Hittite people. These covenants had certain elements that were uniform and very important. They were featured in all covenants back in those days. These elements were:

- *The preamble:* This portion identified the powerful king initiating the covenant and the people who would become his subjects or vassals through the covenant.
- *The historical review:* In this portion the more powerful king listed the many things he had done for the people.

- *Stipulations of the covenant:* These were statements about specific behavior that was expected by each of the two parties in the covenant.
- *Provisions for storage:* In the covenant agreement there were a number of copies of the covenant. This was important so they could be kept and read publicly.
- *Blessings and curses:* Next, associated with the covenant was a list of blessings you could expect if you kept up the covenant and a list of curses for those who broke the covenant.
- *Vow of faithfulness:* This is where people said, "I will be a covenant keeper."

In Exodus, and scattered throughout the whole rest of the Pentateuch, we find every one of these features. God is all about covenant.

What we have to keep in the forefront of our minds is that the laws were never intended to be a list of rules that somebody had to keep to earn salvation. These laws were given after God had redeemed his people from Egypt and called them his beloved children. They were intended to describe *what a covenant relationship with God was supposed to look like.* What would it look like to be a kingdom of priests and a holy nation?

SIGNIFICANT SCRIPTURE

Exodus 20

INTERPRETIVE INSIGHT | Breaking the Law

When we see the Ten Commandments, they tend to be hung on a wall and they read like a list of do's and don'ts. They feel like a list of rules to be followed. The people of Israel would have looked at them differently. They saw a promise of the presence of God. They saw God's copy of his covenant with them. The very first line reads, "I am the LORD *your* God." They carried both copies with them as a reminder of God's loving agreement to be in relationship with them. Were they expected to follow these commandments? Yes! But was God's love for them based on perfect obedience to these commands? No, for he had expressed and promised his love before these laws were given.

With all of this in mind, you can begin to get a picture of what it meant when Israel broke the commands of God. They were not just breeching some little agreement or bending some little rule. They were breaking their covenant with the God who loved them so passionately.

When Israel disobeyed God by making and worshiping the golden calf, do you remember how Moses responded? He smashed the tablets. He shattered them. This was not a thoughtless outburst of anger on his part. The tablets were the visible sign of the covenant. Moses was doing symbolically what the people were doing literally—*breaking the covenant.*

ON THE LIGHTER SIDE | Love and Marriage

Think about a marriage covenant. It needs to begin with a loving and grace-filled commitment, and then actions flow naturally. Suppose a man is dating a woman and things are starting to get to that "serious point." What would happen if he looked deeply into her eyes and said, "O.K., here's the program. I want you to wash my clothes, fix my meals, darn my socks, and clean my house. If you do these things well enough, and I am happy with your performance, then I'll marry you." How would most women respond to this offer?

But once we're married and there is grace-filled love and concern, do you think those actions would just flow naturally? OK, maybe that's not the perfect example, but here is the point. A healthy marriage begins with mutual love and care, then the actions flow out of this love. God's covenant with us is like this. It begins with grace. This was as true in the Old Testament as it is in the New Testament. People have always been saved by grace through faith by trusting in a loving and forgiving God. Then, obedience to his law becomes a response of love to God's goodness. Salvation has never been earned by following certain laws; it has always been by grace.

LIFE APPLICATION | The Concern of God's Heart

God loves us and is deeply concerned about the condition of our hearts and lives. He longs for us to understand that his love for us is not based on our daily performance in keeping every rule and regulation. He wants us to enter into a naturally loving relationship with him.

Sometimes people will think, "I may be living in direct, willful disobedience to God's command, but God owes me a heaven ticket because I walked down the aisle," or, "I prayed a prayer," or, "I signed the card," or "I can pinpoint a date." That's a dangerous road to walk. God is concerned about our heart.

3. Why Is There So Much Detail in the Laws?

Some people read the laws in the Old Testament and wonder, "If God was so concerned about the heart, why did he give so many different laws and why are they so detailed?" The truth is that there are a lot of laws in the Old Testament that can seem very strange to the modern reader. At first glance, someone might think that Moses was an obsessive-compulsive with all these minute details.

But when we look closer, we begin to learn that God had a distinct purpose for every law he gave. Each law, in some way, was a manifestation of God's love and care for his people.

PAUSE FOR REFLECTION
How God Sees My Heart

Take a moment of silence for a heart check. You might want to prompt reflection by asking a few leading questions, such as:

- Are you driven to follow God's commands out of fear and guilt, or out of a deep awareness of his love?
- Are you learning to find joy in following God's commands, or is it always a chore?
- As God looks into your heart today, does he see it full of love for him, partially full, or running dry?

HISTORICAL CONTEXT | Two Tablets

Another indicator that the Ten Commandments were given in the context of God's covenantal grace is seen when we understand the way ancient covenants were preserved. There was always a provision for preserving a copy of a covenant. This was done by making two copies of every covenant—one copy to be kept by each party in the covenant. The king would keep one copy in his "files," the "vassal nation" kept the other one. Without copy machines, it was certainly expensive for two copies to be chiseled onto stone, but that way each party could continually review the covenant they had agreed to, along with its expectations.

When Moses came down from the mountain with the Ten Commandments, how many tablets was he carrying? The answer is, two (Exodus 32:15). Some people think that God ran out of space on the first tablet, so he kept writing on a second one. Others have a picture in their mind of two tablets with five commandments on each of them. But the most likely reason there were two tablets is that God provided a copy for each party, in accordance to the custom of the day. This way, the people of Israel could keep a copy and it could be read and reread publicly. One of the copies belonged to Israel and the other copy belonged to God. But since God lived in the tabernacle in Israel, both copies were kept together.

INTERPRETIVE INSIGHT | Why All These Laws?

The Old Testament has a number of broad laws that make sense to most people. God said things like, "Don't kill each other"; "Don't steal from one another"; "Don't tell lies." We read these, nod our heads, and say, "That makes sense." But, there are a lot of laws that were given for very specific situations. If you're in a certain life situation, you often need a great deal of detail.

SIGNIFICANT SCRIPTURE

Leviticus 11:29–30;
  13:40–41;
Deuteronomy 24:19–22

Here are a few examples of different kinds of laws that had details that can be confusing:

A law about food: Leviticus 11:29–31 says, "Of the animals that move about on the ground, these are unclean for you: the weasel, the rat, any kind of great lizard, the gecko, the monitor lizard, the wall lizard, the skink and the chameleon. Of all those that move along the ground, these are unclean for you. Whoever touches them when they are dead will be unclean till evening."

A law about cleanness: Leviticus 13:40–41 says, "When a man has lost his hair and is bald, he is clean. If he has lost his hair from the front of his scalp and has a bald forehead, he is clean."

A law about farming: Deuteronomy 24:19–22 includes these words, "When you beat the olives from your trees, do not go over a second time."

People look through law after law after law and wonder, "Why are these laws so specific?" If you read through the Pentateuch, you find laws about what to do if someone gets gored by an ox, if a slave gets a tooth knocked out, and who to call if you find a spot of mold on the wall of your house. All these laws can start to feel a little overwhelming!

HISTORICAL CONTEXT | A Barbaric Age

When we look at the detail in the Old Testament laws and the specific nature of so many of them, we need to keep in mind what might be called *"the moral baseline of the human race."* At this time in history, there was no moral or social code to lead human beings. The world we live in today can be very dark and sin-filled, but try to imagine turning the clock back over three thousand years, before there was any influence of the Judeo-Christian ethic. We live with the advantage of over three millennia of the civilizing, restraining, and heart-changing influence of the power of the Ten Commandments.

In the time before God began to give his law, the world was barbaric. Although history teaches us that there were some written moral codes in existence by this time (such as the Code of Hammurabi), it is clear that the world was still in a moral dark age. For instance, infanticide was common. They lived in a world where people routinely sacrificed newborn children to an idol named Molech.

The Old Testament speaks out against sacrifice to Molech. It was a large, hollow, metal statue. When people wanted something from Molech, they would build a fire inside of it and wait until the statue was glowing with heat. Then they would place their child on the arms of the statue. The baby would be seared and burned to death. This religious practice was actually common when God began to give his law.

Slaves were routinely killed with no accountability. Women were largely treated as slaves and possessions. Pagan religions regularly encouraged temple prostitution. When you understand the historical context, you begin to realize that God had to start where the people were, and they were living in a barbaric time.

LIFE APPLICATION | Applying God's Laws

We need to learn how to read the laws in the Bible and discover which ones are meant to be a general rule of life that can be applied in many contexts. Here are some examples that will help us know how to apply the truth of God's laws in daily situations.

Deuteronomy 24:20 speaks of how farmers should deal with their olive harvest. They are told to beat the branches so that olives come down and can be gathered. But they are told not to go back and beat those branches a second time. If there are olives that stay on the tree, just leave them there. Then the text opens our eyes, and hearts, to what God is teaching: "Leave them for the poor so the poor can come through and find something." The principle behind this strange command makes sense to every follower of Christ: Be concerned for the poor; help those in need.

This is the application of a paradigmatic law: "If you're a farmer, be a little sloppy so that the poor can have food." Now, the passage only mentions olive trees. If you had fig trees, you could not say, "Well, the Bible just says olives. It doesn't apply to me because I have fig trees, so I can take down every fig." The judges in Israel would look at the principle involved: "Leave some for the poor." It was a paradigm. It was an example.

The point here is that the law given to Moses by God was never about a narrow, legalistic, nitpicking, rule-keeping mentality. There would be a lot of specific examples so that people would get specific and actually obey God's laws. The laws were meant to transform the hearts of God's people. We need to ask ourselves, "Am I seeking to help those who are poor and outcast?" Or, "Am I living selfishly and providing only for myself? Am I beating the branch twice and leaving nothing for the poor?"

4. How Do We Know Which Laws We Are to Obey?

Some people can look at Christians today and wonder if we simply pick and choose which laws we will follow. Are we arbitrary and self-serving as we choose which laws to follow and which ones no longer apply to us? For instance, most followers of Christ break Old Testament dietary laws every day. We eat things that are forbidden. Also, we fail to follow all the laws for ritual cleansing. Are we being disobedient to God? We need to clarify how we can know which laws in the Old Testament still apply to us today.

WORD STUDY

Paradigmatic Laws

Many of the laws God gave were paradigmatic. This means specific laws gave an example about how to apply a basic life principle. The law may have had a specific application, but a deeper life lesson could touch many more situations than those mentioned in the Bible. In other words, the law was an example, but it was not exhaustive. In our day we try to make laws that will cover virtually every single possible situation. Paradigmatic laws give a general rule that can be applied to countless situations.

SIGNIFICANT SCRIPTURE

Leviticus 19:18;
Deuteronomy 5:17; 6:5; 14:10;
Mark 7; Romans 13:1–7

How Can This Be?

The topic we are addressing is no small issue. How can we know which laws to follow? Just think about it. Deuteronomy 14:10 teaches us that any creature in the water that doesn't have fins or scales, "you may not eat." Yet, many Christians ignore this and sink their teeth into butter-covered lobster and think nothing of it. At the same time, Deuteronomy 5:17 says, "You shall not murder." We seek to uphold this law tenaciously. Both of these commands come from the same book of the Bible. One is widely ignored and the other is upheld in our lives, the church, and society. How can this be?

INTERPRETIVE INSIGHT | Kinds of Laws: Civil and Ceremonial

Since Christ, our relationship to the law has fundamentally changed. The Old Testament law can be put into three general categories. These are not always clear-cut, but the formal distinctions go back to the days of John Calvin.

First of all, some of the Old Testament laws can be called *civil law*. Because Israel was a nation, there were certain laws that had to do with the governance of a people. Things like property rights and sentencing guidelines for the courts (eye for an eye, tooth for a tooth) fall into this category. Now, however, God's people are no longer restricted to one nation. We are scattered throughout all the nations. This means the civil laws about the governance of one particular nation no longer apply to us in the same way. As a matter of fact, the New Testament is clear that followers of Christ ought to follow the laws of the country in which they live and to see those in positions of authority as placed there by God (Romans 13:1–7).

Another kind of law can be called *"ritual law"* or *"ceremonial law."* These are mostly laws about worship, the sacrificial system, or cleanness versus uncleanness. The law of circumcision is an example of ritual law.

In the New Testament the whole sacrificial and ritual system was fulfilled in Christ. He was the ultimate sacrifice and made any continued sacrifices meaningless. All the sacrificial laws came to an end when Jesus died on the cross and rose again. In the same way, all of the laws about ritual cleansing became null and void when Jesus paid the price for our sins and offered cleansing through his shed blood. Ritual cleansing only pointed to Christ. The sacrificial system pointed to Christ. Since he has come, the ceremonial laws are now meaningless and do not need to be followed.

LIFE APPLICATION | Life Lessons for Past Laws

Often there are important principles that can be learned from some of the laws that we no longer need to follow to the letter. Jesus himself spoke directly about this. In Mark 7, for example, he says, "It's not the food that goes into a man that makes him clean or unclean, it's what comes out of his heart." Mark makes a parenthetical comment in Mark 7:19, "In saying this, Jesus declared all foods clean." In other words, Jesus was saying, and Mark makes it explicit, that these old ritual laws about cleanness and uncleanness no longer apply to us.

More than that, Jesus (and Mark) is showing that the categories of clean and unclean things existed to help people develop clean hearts. That's the point, to establish the category of cleanness and rightness, which ultimately impact our hearts. God is still concerned about our hearts, and we should be as well. We may not have to worry about eating something that is categorized as an "unclean" food. But we should always be concerned about what comes out of us. This includes our words and what they communicate to others. It also includes the attitudes and intentions of our hearts. These things matter a great deal to God, and they should matter to us as well.

INTERPRETIVE INSIGHT | Kinds of Laws: Moral

God's concern for the heart can be seen most clearly in the third category of Old Testament law, which is called *"moral law."* The Ten Commandments are a great example of moral laws. Deuteronomy 6:5 ("Love the LORD your God with all your heart and with all your soul and with all your strength") and Leviticus 19:18 ("Love your neighbor as yourself") are also moral laws. These laws apply at all times. They are not ritual laws that have become void through Christ. They are not civil laws that are now replaced by our national civil laws. These are God's moral laws, which will always remain.

We obey these, not as a way to earn God's love, but as a sign of a life built on a covenant relationship with our Creator. The great promise of the Old Testament is that one day these laws will be written on our hearts. God says, through the prophet Jeremiah, "I will put my law in their minds and write it on their hearts" (Jeremiah 31:33). The moral laws apply to all of us, in all situations, at all times!

CREATIVE MESSAGE IDEA | Reading of the Ten Commandments

As a way of honoring God's Word, invite people to stand together and read through the Ten Commandments together. You can make a brief comment after each one or simply have people read them. You can project what they will read onto a screen or have them read out of the Bible, if you provide Bibles that are all the same translation.

Commandment 1: "You shall have no other gods before me."
Comment: God says, "Make following me your top priority above all else."

Commandment 2: "You shall not make for yourself an idol."
Comment: Serve God alone, only God. Don't fixate your eyes or heart on anyone or anything else.

Commandment 3: "You shall not take the name of the LORD your God in vain."
Comment: This commandment applies to profanity, but it is addressing more. It means don't misuse God's name in an oath if you are lying. Don't use spiritual language to cover up a dark heart.

Commandment 4: "Remember the Sabbath day by keeping it holy."
Comment: Honor God by ceasing your constant work and taking time for worship and rest. If God rested on the seventh day, how can we ever hope to press on and never experience Sabbath rest?

Commandment 5: "Honor your father and your mother."
Comment: Even when it's difficult, give them respect, listen to their wisdom, and thank them for all they have done for you.

Commandment 6: "You shall not murder."
Comment: This goes well beyond the prohibition against murdering someone. It means we need to identify and avoid things like tearing people down with our words, hating people in our hearts, and holding grudges. It means we need to learn how to forgive.

Commandment 7: "You shall not commit adultery."
Comment: This includes resisting the temptation to lust and growing in sexual purity.

Commandment 8: "You shall not steal."
Comment: We need to learn to be generous givers and receivers.

Commandment 9: "You shall not bear false witness."
Comment: Be a person of integrity. Let truth flow in every area of your life.

Commandment 10: "You shall not covet."
Comment: Refuse to give in to envy or jealousy. Love people more than their things.

You Will Need
- Someone to lead the congregation in reading the Ten Commandments
- Someone to give a brief word about what these commandments mean to us today after each is read

LIFE APPLICATION | God's Law on Our Hearts

In Exodus 24, after Moses reads "the Book of the Covenant," the people make a vow of faithfulness. In verse 7 the people say, "We will do everything the LORD has said; we will obey." This was a sign of the great hope that one day God's people would obey his commandments in the same way that they obey the law of gravity. It would be natural and normal. At this time they would follow his commands out of hearts overflowing with love.

God's vision for hearts fully devoted to him continues today. He longs for us to learn his moral law and joyfully and willingly to obey it. We need to look at our hearts and make sure that God's law is deep inside of us. Where we are living in disobedience to God's law, we must seek to adjust our lives and attitudes to come in line with God's plan for us.

INTERPRETIVE INSIGHT | A Developmental Process

God takes us through this whole developmental process as he seeks to transform our hearts. All the way back in the Garden of Eden, God gave his commands orally to Adam and Eve. After the Fall took place, God's commands were written down, chiseled in stone and parchment, for his people.

Later in the history of Israel, God sent the prophets to help clarify his teachings and laws. Even later, God sent Jesus so that we could finally see what a life looks like when somebody follows the law of God out of a true response of love. It was Jesus who spoke the words of Matthew 5:17–18 (quoted above). God was developing his people's understanding of that law and how to follow it. At Pentecost, God sent his Holy Spirit to continue speaking the truth of God's law into our hearts. The Spirit still does this today.

All of this developmental process is for us, so that we can have God's magnificent and beautiful law, the intent of God for human life, written in our hearts. It is not given so that we can walk around trying to keep a bunch of mechanical rules to prove how righteous we are. Instead, it is given as a precious gift that will help us grow in a living and loving relationship with our Creator and with each other.

NEW TESTAMENT CONNECTION
Jesus and the Law

Jesus had a lot to say about the law. He set the whole context for his understanding of the law with these words in Matthew 5:17–18:

"Do not think that I have come to abolish the Law or the Prophets; I have not come to abolish them but to fulfill them. I tell you the truth, until heaven and earth disappear, not the smallest letter, not the least stroke of a pen, will by any means disappear from the Law until everything is accomplished."

Jesus was clear that he was going to uphold the law of God, not break it. At the same time, he gave new definition and tone to how we are to understand the law. The people had become legalistic and narrow in their understanding; Jesus brought them back to the heart of what the law was about. In Matthew 5 Jesus gives extended commentary and rabbinic teaching on the Ten Commandments and other laws.

PAUSE FOR REFLECTION | ## What If?

As you close this message, consider inviting people to imagine what life would be like with the full blessing of God's law. Ask people to close their eyes and imagine what our world would be like if, even for one day, everyone on the earth had the law of God written on their hearts and followed it with joy. What if, for one day:

- No life was ended through random violence.

- There were no acts of terrorism.

- Nobody was killed, struck, or even cursed at in anger.

- Not a single lie was told.

- Everyone spoke the truth to one another.

- Every father and every mother were honored all day long, and the hearts of the parents were turned toward their children, and the hearts of the children were turned toward their parents.

- Nothing was stolen.

- Not one greedy thought or action took place in all the earth.

What would the world be like if God's magnificent law were written on our hearts and we lived them out in our lives? What if we lived the kind of life Jesus did right in our home, our work place, our school, and our church?

As you close the message, invite people to consider living out that dream in their lives. Pray for each person gathered to begin walking in the dream, because God wants to make it a reality.

Lessons from the Wilderness

EXODUS 3; 13–16; 32–33; NUMBERS 11–13; DEUTERONOMY 8

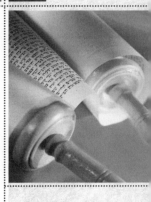

The Heart of the
MESSAGE

The wisest people learn from the example of others. Sometimes the lessons learned show the path to life. At other times, these lessons show us which paths to avoid. As we look at the people of Israel in their wilderness wanderings, we learn from their victories and their failures. In this message, God will invite us to grow in wisdom as we learn from those who have gone before us. Their pitfalls can be avoided. Their victories can be repeated. We can grow as we walk through the wilderness experiences of our lives.

God kept his people in the wilderness because there were certain lessons they needed to learn. The wilderness doesn't provide a lot of distractions. In the wilderness, people are a lot more likely to pay attention to God. It is a furnace where God can refine, melt, purify, and shape his people into who he wants them to be. Throughout the history of the Old Testament many of God's most important people spent time in the wilderness furnace: Moses, David, Elijah, and the entire nation of Israel. God still invites those he loves to his wilderness school.

The Heart of the
MESSENGER

In this message you will study eight different life lessons drawn from the wilderness time in the history of Israel. As you prepare to communicate these lessons to God's people, ask the Holy Spirit to speak to your heart about which lessons you need to learn today. Seek to identify one key lesson that really hits home for you. How does this lesson affirm a positive direction you are taking in your journey toward God? How does it uncover ways you are wandering away from God's plan for your life? What adjustments do you need to make in order to align your life and attitudes with God's plan for you according to what you learn through this wilderness lesson?

Brief Message OUTLINE

1 A lesson about God
2 A lesson about remembering
3 A lesson about attitude
4 A lesson about perspective
5 A lesson about manna (provision)
6 A lesson about presence
7 A lesson about humility
8 A lesson about fear and faith

Sermon Introduction

In the sermon introduction, you can use one or more of several video clips, contained on the CD-ROM, as creative message ideas.

Wilderness Lesson 1: A Lesson about God

NARRATIVE ON THE TEXT | Map Time

(For this section you will need the Power Point slides provided on the CD-ROM.)

To help people get a sense of the travel route the people of Israel took to get from Egypt to the Promised Land, consider using the maps provided in the Power Point presentation. You can put the trip in your own words or use the narrative provided below.

The trip the people of Israel were to take was quite a simple one. They were in Egypt and were going to go to Canaan. If you take a look on the screen, you will see the simplest route, called the Way of the Sea. God says, "I've come to bring them out of Egypt into a good and spacious land flowing with milk and honey."

As you look at the map, it looks like a really simple trip from Egypt to the Promised Land. The only bad thing is they have to go through the Sinai Peninsula, which was not pleasant. But it is not a long trip, only about two hundred miles from Goshen in the land of Egypt to where the Israelites are heading in Canaan, and they all know the best route to get there.

Everybody knows the shortest distance between two points is a straight line. There was pretty much a straight road between these two locations in those days. It was an international trade route called the Way of the Philistines. It was a real road. In Isaiah 9:1 it's called the Way of the Sea. It was kind of the scenic route, because it went right along the Mediterranean Sea. You can see it on the map. The people of Israel knew that this would be the natural and quickest way to go. It would be a short trip—a matter of weeks—not months, but weeks.

SIGNIFICANT SCRIPTURE

Exodus 3:7–10; 13:17–18; Deuteronomy 1:2

CREATIVE MESSAGE IDEA | "What's Up" Video Clip

In each of the video kits there will be one "What's Up" video piece. This is a light and often humorous way to help people learn that asking questions is good. You can use this video piece here (or any other week you feel it fits). We have placed it here so that you have a video every other week, but this piece is not bound thematically to any particular week of the Old Testament Challenge.

You Will Need
• Video projection capability in your worship center
• Someone to run the video during the service

But, surprisingly, in Exodus 13:17–18 we are told that God has decided on a different route:

> When Pharaoh let the people go, God did not lead them on the road through the Philistine country, though that was shorter. For God said, "If they face war, they might change their minds and return to Egypt." So God led the people around by the desert road toward the Red Sea. The Israelites went up out of Egypt armed for battle.

The desert road was heavily strategic and heavily fortified. The Egyptians had a large military presence there. God knew the hearts of his people. He knew they were timid and easily frightened. He knew that they did not have much faith. He knew that if they ran into much opposition, they would turn around and go back to Egypt and be slaves again. So he did not send them along the Way of the Sea, even though it was the fastest and most direct route.

There was another road that cut pretty much through the center of the Sinai Peninsula. It ran east and west. It would have been a little more out of the way, but much safer. However, God did not send them on that road either.

There was a third road that went almost directly south, called the Way of the Wilderness. This was the road that God led them down after they crossed the Red Sea. If you look on the map, you will see that this road went all the way down to Mount Sinai.

Nobody knows exactly where Mount Sinai was located, but the general consensus among scholars is that it was located down somewhere in the southern tip of the Sinai Peninsula as pictured on the map. Once they traveled to Mount Sinai, the Israelites were there for about a year. Look at it this way: The first leg of the Israelites' journey was a two-week trip that took them one year.

Finally it was time to break camp, and the pillar of cloud and fire was going to lead them onward to the Promised Land. They took a road called the Mount Seir Road, or the Road to Kadesh Barnea. It went from the tip of the Sinai Peninsula to Canaan. We know how long this journey took because

---

CREATIVE MESSAGE IDEA | Drama on Video: "Mysterious Ways"

This video drama is on the OTC video tape for kit 1. It is six minutes and forty-five seconds long and can be used at whatever point in the worship service it fits best. You will want to review it in advance to find the best place it fits, perhaps even in the midst of the message.

You Will Need
• The ability to show a video tape during your service
• Someone to run the video for you

Deuteronomy 1:2 says: "It takes eleven days to go from Horeb [Horeb is another name for Mount Sinai] to Kadesh Barnea by the Mount Seir road." This time an eleven-day trip took thirty-nine years!

INTERPRETIVE INSIGHT | God Is Not in a Hurry

There is a huge spiritual lesson in the travel plans God had for Israel: God is not in a hurry! God's primary concern is not speed. Ours usually is. God knew that *where* the people of Israel were going was not nearly as important as *who* they were becoming. God knew that possessing a land flowing with milk and honey was not nearly as important as having a heart flowing with love, justice, courage, and faith. God's first concern was not how fast his people would be going to the Promised Land. His deepest concern was that they would be the right kind of people once they arrived. If it took forty years to prepare their hearts, then so be it!

ILLUSTRATION | Are We There Yet?

Anytime a family goes on vacation and they have little kids in the backseat, the little kids will ask a question. They ask it often. They ask it irritatingly. They sometimes turn it into a chant or a song. The longer the trip is, the sooner they start with the question. And the question, of course, is: "Are we there yet?"

Parents look forward to the day when kids mature and become patient and there's no more silly fighting over space violations, no more arguing over what radio station should get played, no more whining about where or when they're going to stop for lunch. They wait a long time for that day to come because, although most of us grow up, we never get much different.

ON THE LIGHTER SIDE | When Will the Hurrying End?

From our youngest days we begin the frenzied and hurried pace. We push forward and keep crying out, "Are we there yet?" Parents are in a hurry for their little one to take their first step, speak their first word, and catch their first ball. Soon the child learns the hurry game.

"When do I start school? Am I there yet?"
"When will I be grown up? Am I there yet?"
"When will I fall in love? Am I there yet?"

"When will I get out of school? Am I there yet?"
"When can I move out? Am I there yet?"
"When will I get married? Am I there yet?"
"When will I get the perfect job? Am I there yet?"
"When can I retire? Am I there yet?"
"When will I die? Am I there yet?"

If we are not careful, we can rush from the cradle to the grave and forget that God has plans for us today!

LIFE APPLICATION | Still in a Hurry

As we grow older, we discover that our childlike chant "Are we there yet?" continues with some subtle adjustments. Now it sounds like this:

"God, get me into this job and do it now."

"Get me into this house, I need it soon."

"Get me into this relationship, I can't wait."

"Get me into this financial condition, I can't hold on any longer."

"Are we there yet? Are we there yet? Are we there yet?"

What God knew for the people of Israel, he still knows for us today. Having a portfolio flowing with dollars or a job flowing with power doesn't matter nearly as much as having a character that flows with the fruit of the Spirit. God is still more concerned with who we are becoming than how quickly we get to our desired location.

NEW TESTAMENT CONNECTION | God and Time

We have a certain way of looking at time. Our perspective is limited because we live within the confines of space and time. God has a radically different vantage point. He created time and space, and he is not subject to their limitations. This is why the apostle Peter writes, "But do not forget this one thing, dear friends: With the Lord a day is like a thousand years, and a thousand years are like a day" (2 Peter 3:8). We might be in a hurry, but God has a better view than we do: He created time, so we can trust him to lead us in his timing.

PAUSE FOR REFLECTION

Time to Slow Down

Allow a time for silence and encourage people to take an honest inventory of their lives. Where are we rushing? What is our destination? Are we rushing to arrive but forgetting to walk with God along the way? How can we slow down to notice God, hear his voice, and respond to his leading in our lives?

Here is a thought for reflection for you as a teacher. As you prepare this message and bring it to God's people, be sure you take time to slow down and meet with God. You might even want to consider prayerfully choosing only selected lessons from this message as you teach. If your time constraints will not allow you to address all eight lessons effectively, teach only those that will connect most closely with the needs of your congregation—and do so slowly.

ON THE LIGHTER SIDE | A Day and a Thousand Years

We get very anxious about time. God has a different perspective. This humorous story makes the point and gives a lighter look at God and time.

A little boy (or girl) was praying after his Sunday school lesson. He said, "Dear God, I hear that time is very different for you than it is for us. Is that true?"

God said, "Yes, my child, that is very true."

The boy continued, "What is a thousand years like to you?"

"It is like a second," God replied.

"Then what is a second like?" the boy asked.

"It is like a thousand years."

This got the boy thinking. The little wheels in his head really got spinning. "God, what is a million dollars like to you?"

God answered, "It is like a penny."

The boy asked, "Then what is a penny like to you?"

"It is like a million dollars."

The boy paused and then asked his final question, "Dear God, can I please have a penny?"

God answered, "Yes! I'll give you a penny, but you'll have to wait for a second!"

Wilderness Lesson 2: A Lesson about Remembering

INTERPRETIVE INSIGHT | Being Intentional about Remembering

SIGNIFICANT
SCRIPTURE

Exodus 15:22–24;
Psalm 136

We need to be intentional about remembering what God has done and who he is. The Israelites have just been delivered from Pharaoh and his army. They have crossed the Red Sea, and God has given them miraculous redemption. The mighty hand of God has been revealed in power through plagues, a pillar of fire, and deliverance from the hand of the most powerful ruler on the face of the earth! It would seem that this manifestation of God's presence and power would leave a lasting and indelible impression on the people of Israel. It would be natural to think that the impact of these events would stay with them forever. But notice how quickly they forget. In just three days they are discouraged, grumbling, and angry.

It took only three days for the people to forget all that God had done for them. You might think that since God has just delivered them from Egypt, performed the ten plagues, and drowned Pharaoh and his army in the Red Sea that their faith might be unshakable. But just three days later God is at the wheel driving and the kids are in the backseat whining and complaining. They have forgotten. Their short memory is evidence of the fact that they have missed the profound spiritual reality that *God is with them*.

LIFE APPLICATION | Setting Up Memorials

All through the Old Testament, God called the people of Israel to remember what he had done for them. One of the practical reminders was setting up a pile of stones as a memorial so that they would see this visible sign and remember what God had done for them (Joshua 4:4–7). We, like the people of Israel, are prone to forget. We need to learn how to set up piles of stones that will remind us of the great things God has done for us.

Maybe we don't actually pile up rocks, but there are ways we can remember God's goodness in our past. Some people keep a list of answered prayers to remind them of God's power and faithfulness. Others make a point of retelling stories of what God has done in their past (Psalm 136). There are people who will capture a great moment of spiritual growth or learning with a photograph they display or in a poem or picture they have drawn. The key concern is not *what* we use as a reminder as much as *that* we remember God's goodness in our lives.

Wilderness Lesson 3: A Lesson about Attitude

INTERPRETIVE INSIGHT | Prone to Grumble

We are all prone to grumble, but we must fight against this temptation. When the people of Israel come to Marah and find that the water is bitter, they begin to grumble and complain. They forget God's mighty acts and focus only on their thirst. Even though their attitudes are poor, God miraculously provides. He tells Moses to throw a piece of wood into the water, and when Moses does, the water becomes pure.

Now it would seem that the people of Israel have everything they need. Let's do a quick inventory:

* They have freedom from the oppression of Egypt.

* They have miraculous guidance and direction through God's presence in a pillar of cloud and fire.

* They have supernatural water to drink.

With all of this going for the people of Israel, we would expect to see them faithful to God and content with his provision. But there is one theme, one key word that jumps out of this story over and over again. Read Exodus 16:6–12 and ask those listening to identify the word that seems to come through again and again. It's the word "grumble."

LIFE APPLICATION | Yes, It Is a Sin!

Grumbling is a sin! There is no question about it. Although we often don't see it as a big deal, God does. Grumbling causes division and conflict in homes and churches. This is a sin that God wants to be purged from our lives.

We need to look at our own lives and be sure we have not fallen into patterns of grumbling and complaining. It is helpful for every follower of Christ to do an occasional attitude check and make sure a grumbling spirit has not begun to grow in our hearts. If you are the courageous type, you might even want to ask a close friend or family member if they see any patterns of grumbling and complaining in your life.

> *Always speaking well of the deserving,*
> *but never ill of the undeserving,*
> *we shall attain to the glory and Kingdom of God.*
>
> IRENAEUS (SECOND CENTURY)

SIGNIFICANT SCRIPTURE

Exodus 15:22–24; 16:6–12

NEW TESTAMENT CONNECTION

A Lesson for Generations to Come

God is so concerned about the sin of grumbling that he lists it alongside idolatry, sexual immorality, and testing God (1 Corinthians 10:6–10) as the sins of God's people while they were in the wilderness. The apostle Paul is clear that the history of Israel in the wilderness serves as a reminder of some things we should *not* do. Paul puts it this way: "Now these things occurred as examples to keep us from setting our hearts on evil things as they did."

Wilderness Lesson 4: A Lesson about Perspective

INTERPRETIVE INSIGHT | On Discontent

SIGNIFICANT SCRIPTURE

Exodus 16:1-3

Discontent distorts our perspective and twists our view of reality. In Exodus 16 we see how the entire perspective of the Israelites becomes warped. In their discontent, they begin to rewrite their history. Discontent can distort our perspective and play with our mind. We begin to maximize how bad our present condition is, and we look with rose-colored glasses at how things used to be or at how things are for somebody else. That's just human nature. That's what's going on with the people of Israel.

Note Exodus 16:3: "If only we had died by the LORD's hand in Egypt!" These people are raising complaint to an art form. "We're not asking for much," they say, "just death. There in Egypt we sat around pots of meat and ate all the food we wanted."

Think for a moment about what their occupation was in Egypt. They were slaves! They did not sit around having fondue all day long when they were in Egypt. They were in forced servitude, they were being beaten, they were miserable! But now, discontent about their present situation allows them to see their past in a distorted light. That's what discontent can do.

ON THE LIGHTER SIDE | What Is It?

This name "manna" becomes kind of an inside joke to the Israelites. In the Hebrew language, manna simply means "what is it?" They didn't know exactly what this stuff was, so they called it manna. Can you imagine the conversation in the morning? "What do you want for breakfast?" "I'll have a bowl of 'what is it?'"

For a little more information on manna, read Exodus 16:14, "When the dew was gone, thin flakes like frost on the ground appeared on the desert floor." This was the introduction of the first breakfast cereal, Frosted Flakes. When the Israelites first started eating the manna, they thought it was Grrrrrrreat! Sadly, after a short time they even complained about this provision from God.

Wilderness Lesson 5: A Lesson about (Manna) Provision

INTERPRETIVE INSIGHT | Living One Day at a Time

We are invited into a journey of living one day at a time. The people have grumbled and complained. They have become discontent and have begun to look back on the "glory days" of Egypt. We might expect God to get upset, impatient, or even angry, but he is very gracious. He just keeps providing. God gives the people meat in the form of quail and bread in the form of manna.

God's provision is wonderful. It is exactly what they needed and there is enough for everyone. Every day, one day at a time, God gives what his people need. In an interesting twist, anytime the people gather more than they need and try to stockpile it for the next day, it goes rotten and is filled with maggots. They can only gather what they need for the day. Then, to the amazement of all the people, when they gather twice as much as they need before the Sabbath (as God commands), the manna stays fresh.

INTERPRETIVE INSIGHT | All You Need

What is God trying to teach his people? Moses makes this explicit in Deuteronomy 8:3 when he looks back on this episode decades later. He says, "God humbled you, causing you to hunger and then fed you with manna." God was teaching his people to depend on him, one day at a time. They could not rely on their own strength, their own wisdom, or their own resources. In the desert they learned that all they needed could be found in the hands of the God who had formed them.

SIGNIFICANT SCRIPTURE

Exodus 16; Deuteronomy 8:1–5

All we want in Christ, we shall find in Christ. If we want little, we shall find little. If we want much, we shall find much; but if, in utter helplessness, we cast our all on Christ, he will be to us the whole treasury of God.

HENRY BENJAMIN WIPPLE

ON THE LIGHTER SIDE | A Divine Tailor

God provided more than just food for his children as they wandered in the desert. In Deuteronomy 8:4 we read, "Your clothes did not wear out and your feet did not swell." In other words, shoes and sandals were provided as well. Think of what forty years of constant marching, blazing sun, and howling sandstorms would do to clothes. Do you think they ran into a lot of K-Marts out in the desert? As God provided through divine power, their clothes did not wear out. Moses said, "You didn't get your clothes from Lord and Taylor. The Lord was your tailor." That's the way it worked in the desert. God was saying to his people, "I'll take care of you. I'm enough. Trust me."

A Prayer for Manna

Take a moment to pray for each person gathered to begin living by the manna principle. Also, allow a time of silence where they can pray for God to give them a new trust for the daily manna that only God can provide.

You might even want to use the brief prayer provided below:

God, give me manna for today, just this day. Give me enough wisdom. Give me enough patience. Give me enough courage. Give me enough love to handle this day. And as best I can, God, I'll trust that when I wake up in the morning, you'll be there with me and you'll help me face tomorrow. I'm not going to try to collect more from you than I need. I want to learn to trust you for this day.

LIFE APPLICATION | ## The Manna Principle

Here is the manna principle: *one day at a time.* God will provide for you one day at a time. Trust God for this day right now. Some of the Israelites got anxious. Some got greedy. Some got afraid. Some thought they'd beat the system by gathering tomorrow's manna. God had something important to teach them—and us as well. It is the manna principle by which we are to live. God says, "I want you to live your life trusting me one day at a time—just this day. Learn to trust me for this day. If you start worrying about tomorrow, you are going to worry your whole life long."

We don't need to ask for guarantees about tomorrow. We don't need to ask for answers to questions we are not being asked yet. We don't need to ask for the ability to cross a bridge that we haven't yet reached. We need to learn to pray, "God, I'll trust you for this day, my daily bread, today. When I wake up tomorrow morning, like manna, your mercies will be new once again."

NEW TESTAMENT CONNECTION | ## Our Daily Bread

Jesus lived with an understanding of the Father's daily provision and called his followers to do the same. When he taught his disciples the essential life prayer (often called the Lord's Prayer), he told them to pray, "Give us today our daily bread" (Matthew 6:11). That's the manna principle. That's the way Jesus lived. That's the way we should live.

Wilderness Lesson 6: A Lesson about Presence

INTERPRETIVE INSIGHT | Life Choices

SIGNIFICANT SCRIPTURE

Exodus 17:7; 32:1–21; 33:12–17; Psalm 84:10

We can choose to walk in the real and life-changing presence of God or we can cling to lifeless idols. The people of Israel ask a fundamental question that goes through all of our minds at one point or another in our lives: "Is the LORD among us or not?" (Exodus 17:7).

When we hear the Israelites ask this question, it seems unbelievable. After all God has done—the ten plagues, the parting of the Red Sea, the deliverance from Pharaoh, the destruction of the Egyptian army, the provision of manna and water—they still dare to ask this question: "Is the Lord really among us?"

But before we come down too hard on them, we need to look at our own lives. God is so powerful, he is so present, and yet we dare to wonder if he will continue to be with us. We, like the people of Israel, need to learn that God is with us, even when we are too blind to see him and too hardhearted to feel his presence.

NARRATIVE ON THE TEXT | Unwilling to Wait

Even though God's people question his presence, once more he is patient. Once more he provides. He leads them to Mount Sinai, and Moses is called to meet God on the mountain for forty days and forty nights. All the people have to do is wait. That's all they have to do—just wait. They're not hungry; they've got manna. They're not thirsty; they've got water. All they have to do is wait—they just need to have enough faith to wait.

In Exodus 32:1 we read, "When the people saw that Moses was so long in coming down from the mountain, they gathered around Aaron and said, 'Come, make us gods who will go before us. As for this fellow Moses . . . '" Notice the language here. "This fellow" is kind of a distancing thing. "Where's what's-his-name—Moses?" "As for this fellow Moses who brought us up out of Egypt, we don't know what has happened to him."

So the people cry out to Aaron, "Make us gods who will go before us." They don't want to wait. They're not interested in God's timing. They don't understand that God has good reasons for wanting them to be rooted where they are for awhile. They just want to get out of this desert and get to the milk-and-honey place. We can hear their voices crying through history, "Are we there yet?"

A Hunger for God's Presence

Moses makes a beautiful request of God in Exodus 33:15: "Then Moses said to him, 'If your Presence does not go with us, do not send us up from here.'" In other words, Moses says, "You know, God, even though you're offering to send us to a promised land that's flowing with milk and honey, and even though you will give us security, peace, and affluence, we need more. Even though you have given us the Ten Commandments and all the moral guidance we could ever need, there is still something we need. We need your Presence with us!"

Moses is saying that he would rather live in a desert with God than live in the Promised Land with abundance, affluence, security, and protection, but without God's presence.

Pause for a time of silent reflection and encourage people to reflect on areas of their lives where God's presence has not been welcome. Take time to ask God to fill these areas with his presence in new, fresh, and powerful ways.

INTERPRETIVE INSIGHT | Commandments Given and Broken

The people of God are unwilling to wait forty days. They want to control God rather than have him lead them. They prefer to have a golden calf they can manipulate than a living God they have to obey. A lot of us are like that. With an idol, a golden calf, we get our way. With God, we must listen and follow his way. Amazingly, Aaron gives in. He knows better, but he won't stand up to them. As a result, he fashions a golden calf and gives it to the people.

There is tremendous irony in this story. Moses is on the mountaintop receiving the Ten Commandments from God and making a covenant with God. Simultaneously, while that is happening, the "people of the covenant" are down below worshiping an idol and engaging in the kind of sexually abhorrent practices that God was trying to purge from the human race.

LIFE APPLICATION | Taking Responsibility

We learn another key lesson from Israel in Exodus 32. It is a lesson about taking responsibility. That's always the struggle for human beings. We have seen this ever since the Garden of Eden when God came to Adam and said, "Adam, did you eat the fruit?" And Adam said, "Ask the woman that you gave me."

Here Moses confronts Aaron. Exodus 32:21 says, "Moses said to Aaron, 'What did these people do to you, that you led them into such great sin?'" In other words, there must have been some horrible coercion, some terrible threat, physical pressure, something.

"'Do not be angry, [now notice this phrase] my lord,' Aaron answered." Now remember, Moses is Aaron's brother. Do you ever call your brother, "My lord"? He's laying it on a little thick because he's trying to appease Moses. "'Do not be angry, my lord,' Aaron answered. 'You know how prone these people are to evil.'"

Now look at the follow-up excuse Aaron tries to use. "They said to me, 'Make us gods who will go before us. As for this fellow Moses who brought us up out of Egypt, we don't know what has happened to him.' So I told them, 'Whoever has any gold jewelry, take it off.' Then they gave me the gold, and I threw it into the fire, and out came this calf!"

In other words, "It's unbelievable! You should have been there. I've never seen anything like it. In goes the gold and out pops the calf." It's the same old tendency—an inability or refusal to say, "This is what I did. Here's my part. I am responsible."

As we walk through the Old Testament Challenge, we will see many examples of people who refuse to take personal responsibility for their sinful actions. We need to learn from their bad example and choose not to respond in the same manner. We need to identify where we have sinned and confess honestly. This is the way to healing and hope.

Wilderness Lesson 7: A Lesson about Humility

NARRATIVE ON THE TEXT | ### Celebrate

We need to celebrate God's work in and through others. Two men in the camp of Israel begin to prophesy. Their names are Eldad and Medad. Up to this point Moses was the one who did this. All of a sudden, the Spirit descends on these two men out of the blue, and they begin to speak prophetic words. When this happens, Joshua tells Moses to make them stop. In Joshua's mind, only Moses is supposed to prophesy. It is one of the things that makes Moses special. And since Joshua is Moses' assistant, it makes Joshua special. But if everybody is going to start prophesying, then Moses and Joshua won't be special anymore.

Moses looks at things differently from Joshua. Joshua says, "Moses, my lord, stop them!" Moses, says, "Are you jealous for my sake? I wish that all of the LORD's people were prophets and that the LORD would put his Spirit on them!" The humility of Moses shows through, and we can almost hear him say, "I really don't want to be more special, more unique, or more spiritual than anybody. I wish that God would put his Spirit on everyone."

LIFE APPLICATION | ### Time to Celebrate

We need to get serious and intentional about celebrating the way God works in and through the lives of others. It would be a great practice for every follower of Jesus to make a regular habit of celebrating God's work in the people around them. Speak a word of affirmation, write an encouraging note, or even give a small gift to celebrate a specific way you see God working in the life of another person.

> **SIGNIFICANT SCRIPTURE**
>
> Numbers 11:26-29

Nothing sets a person so much out of the devil's reach as humility.

JONATHAN EDWARDS
(EIGHTEENTH CENTURY)

Wilderness Lesson 8: A Lesson about Fear and Faith

NARRATIVE ON THE TEXT | The Good News and the Bad News

Moses sends out twelve spies, and they are gone for forty days. They come back and file their report. Look at Numbers 13:27: "They gave Moses this account: 'We went into the land to which you sent us, and it does flow with milk and honey!'" It's a land of abundance. They are clear that the reports of the amazing bounty of this land were not exaggerated!

However, they also point out that the people who live there are big and strong. The cities are fortified. They want Moses and all of the people to know that this is a really dangerous place. Ten of the spies bring a bad report and discourage the people from even trying to go in and take the land.

Now two of the spies, Joshua and Caleb, give a dissenting report. Numbers 13:30 says: "Then Caleb silenced the people before Moses and said, 'We should go up and take possession of the land, for we can certainly do it.'" But the people in the wilderness school don't believe this. They don't believe that God's protection will be enough for them. They refuse to enter.

INTERPRETIVE INSIGHT | Fear and Faith

Fear robs us of joy and the potential of walking with God to new and exciting places. *Faith* leads us on an exciting journey of daily trust in God. Numbers 13:32–33 contains a poignant image. The ten spies with the bad report say, "We can't attack those people; they are stronger than we are." And they also say, "The land we explored devours those living in it. All the people we saw there are of great size. We saw the Nephilim there (the descendants of Anak come from the Nephilim). We seemed like grasshoppers in our own eyes, and we looked the same to them."

Here's the sentence that reveals the power of fear: "We seemed like grasshoppers in our own eyes." Not only did the spies feel like grasshoppers with no strength. They let the poison of their fear spread through the people of Israel until they all had a grasshopper complex.

Many of these people have never really recovered from the "slave mentality" they learned in their years of bondage in Egypt. As far back as they can remember, all they have ever been is somebody's slave—no dreams, no power. The tragedy is that this generation will never see themselves as anything but grasshoppers. They will not allow hope and joy to fill their hearts. They will not allow themselves to trust God for the great adventure he wants to lead them through.

SIGNIFICANT SCRIPTURE

Numbers 13

God wants his children to follow him in faith. He wants us to trust his provision, his power, and his faithfulness. When we do, we will enter a life of joy and a journey of faith beyond our wildest dreams.

Faith is . . . believing what you do not yet see;
its reward is to see what you believe.

AUGUSTINE (FIFTH CENTURY)

LIFE APPLICATION | Walking in Faith

But God does not desert his people. He waits with the Israelites in the desert for forty years. He holds them in his arms while a new generation grows up—a generation that will walk by faith into God's plan. He forgives them. He stays with them. He keeps watch over them. He keeps the manna supply going.

What is sad to realize is that the present generation never knows what might have been. They miss the adventure of what it could have been to enter the Promised Land of God. It is their children who will see this dream become a reality.

God wants us to be a generation of risk-taking, faith-filled adventurers. God is asking us to do something new and fresh. Maybe it's an involvement in ministry. Maybe it's leading a small group. Maybe it's a new level of commitment with your family. Maybe it's a financial adventure in giving with a new level of sacrifice and joy. Whatever it is, make the commitment to walk by faith and enter the blessing of being in the center of God's will.

PAUSE FOR REFLECTION

I'm No Grasshopper

Some people live with a deep-seated grasshopper complex. If the truth were known, they would say, "I look in the mirror, and all I see is a grasshopper. I'm not adequate. I'm not competent. I'm not strong enough." They live with the daily pain of feeling deeply inferior. But the issue isn't whether we are adequate or competent or strong enough. The question is: Are we willing to trust God one day at a time?

Take time for silent reflection so that people can identify areas of life where they live with fear and feelings of incompetence. Challenge them to meditate on the reality that God's power in them is enough to bring hope and strength to overcome.

What Indiana Jones Was Looking For

EXODUS 24–30; LEVITICUS 16

The Heart of the
MESSAGE

You can tell a lot about people by where they live. If you get a chance to visit someone's home and do a brief walk-through, you can gain insight into their values, loves, and priorities. For better or for worse, we make pretty strong judgments and decisions about a person based on the environment where they live.

In this message, we will look at the house of God. In the Pentateuch we learn about God's choice to live among his people. His dwelling place, the tabernacle, gives us amazing insight into the heart of God and how he relates with his children.

The Heart of the
MESSENGER

As you prepare to bring this message, take time to walk around your home and reflect on what you see. What do you learn about your values, priorities, and passions? Let this experience help shape how you look at the passages in this week's message. The tabernacle, with all its furnishings, points to God's values, priorities, and passions. After you have surveyed your home and God's dwelling place as shown in these passages, think about how you might change the furnishings in your home (literally or spiritually) to line up your life more closely with God's priorities for you.

Introduction

Most of us dream about the kind of place we'd like to live in someday. There are all kinds of magazines, TV shows, web sites, and books devoted to home building and improvement. Our homes take up a good amount of our time and finances. Even with all we put into them, most of us still have a list of changes we want to make and things we want to fix. For some of us, this list gets longer and longer as the years pass. If we look at our home and our plans for improvement, we can learn a lot about what matters to us.

ON THE LIGHTER SIDE | ## In a Van Down by the River

There was a character on a television show some years ago who had a unique home situation that spoke volumes about him. He was a "wannabe" motivational speaker, but life was not going well. He always ended up reflecting on his problems, plight, and present life situation, and his final line would always be a summary of his housing situation (a metaphor for his whole life): "I live in a van down by the river." Let's be honest, who is going to listen to a motivational speaker who is living in a van down by the river?

CREATIVE MESSAGE IDEA | ## A Look at Houses

Set a table (or a number of tables) in the entry area to your church. Cover these tables with magazines that focus on homes and home repair. You might even invite people to bring these kinds of magazines the week before, but don't tell them why. Just ask them to bring them and place them on the tables as they enter. Set a placard on each table with just one question, "What do you learn about a person's character and priorities by looking at their house?" As people come in, they can browse through a couple of magazines and begin making the connection between houses and the people who live in the house.

You Will Need

- Tables set up near the entry area of your church
- An announcement about bringing magazines (a week early)
- Magazines for the tables
- Placards on the tables

1. The Tabernacle

INTERPRETIVE INSIGHT | God Is with Us

The instructions for what God's dwelling place should look like begin in Exodus 25. Take a moment to read Exodus 24:17–18, "To the Israelites the glory of the LORD looked like a consuming fire on top of the mountain. Then Moses entered the cloud as he went on up the mountain. And he stayed on the mountain forty days and forty nights."

During this specific time when the people of God were at Mount Sinai, they saw God's presence, and it was glorious. It was like a cloud on the mountain. You can be sure they would have loved to see that glory stay in such a powerful and visible way, but it did not.

God wanted his people to know he would be with them, even when the mountain was not consumed in fire, so he showed them a new way to know he was with them. In Exodus 25, God begins to give instructions about the building of the tabernacle, his dwelling place. Exodus 25:8 helps us understand the reason God wanted a tabernacle to be built: "Then have them make a sanctuary for me, and I will dwell among them." The key word is "dwell." The tabernacle was a visible sign of the presence of God with his people. When the people of God saw the tabernacle, they could say, "God is with us!"

INTERPRETIVE INSIGHT | A Meeting Place

It is as if God is telling Moses that the people need a physical reminder that he is with them. They need a place that will be full of details and activities that will teach them about God's character and will and about how they can relate to him. So God tells Moses to build a tent (tabernacle) in the middle of the camp. Specifically, the people of Israel are to build a courtyard, and in the courtyard a tent, and in the tent a compartment called the Most Holy Place. In that compartment they are to put a box called an ark.

God says, as we will see, "I will come and meet with you on top of that box, and I will provide manna for you every morning, and I will give you water to drink. I will lead you through the desert from one river to another." And the God of the universe says, "I will live in a tent out in the desert just so I can be with my people." All this detail, all the instructions, is given so that the people can have a place to meet with their God.

SIGNIFICANT SCRIPTURE

Exodus 24–27;
Leviticus 26:11

WORD STUDY

Tabernacle

The word "dwell" (Exodus 25:8) has a specific meaning. In the Hebrew language it is the same word as that used for a tabernacle. It's a little like our modern word "tent." It could be used as a noun or a verb. Literally, Exodus 25:8 could be translated that God is saying, "I will tabernacle with my people." As we see the word "tabernacle," we need to understand that it is not just the word used for the place (the tent) in the middle of the camp of Israel. It is also the word that describes what God was doing. His activity was, and is, to tabernacle (dwell) among his people.

*The best way to prepare for the coming of Christ
is to never forget the presence of Christ.*

WILLIAM BARCLAY

LIFE APPLICATION | Learning to Dwell with God

As we study the tabernacle, we are really studying how we can learn to dwell with God. The tabernacle gives powerful insight and instruction that helps us learn to enter a new and rich relationship with our Creator. As we begin to walk through the tabernacle toward the dwelling place of God, we need to realize that our attitude and heart condition influence the process.

God tells Moses in Exodus 25:2: "Tell the Israelites to bring me an offering. You are to receive the offering for me from each man whose heart prompts him to give." Everybody can be part of making a place where they can meet with God, but it will be strictly voluntary. God gives the invitation, but the people must respond. This is true for us today as well. God invites us to places of intimacy with him, but we have to hear his invitation and enter in.

INTERPRETIVE INSIGHT | Hearts Overflowing

Exodus 36:3–6 tells us that the hearts of the people were so moved that they just kept bringing offerings day after day. They could not stop themselves; they kept on giving. Finally, it got to the point where Moses had to give a command that the people stop giving. Their hearts were overflowing with love so much that they gave more than was needed!

PAUSE FOR PRAYER

Draw Me Close

Pause to pray that each person present will hunger more for God's presence. Invite each person to quietly ask God to help them draw near. If there are things standing in the way, ask for the Holy Spirit to come and begin a process of removing those things.

ON THE LIGHTER SIDE | Joyful Extravagance

The tabernacle was made of the finest materials available, including a lot of gold and silver. We know that God does not need precious metals. They are no more rare to him than tin or bronze. But the use of these had specific significance. To put it in a contemporary context, if you're a man and you've ever had a wife or a girlfriend, you might know what it feels like to buy flowers for her. Why does one person spend a big chunk of cash on a dozen red roses? Is there anything strategic about a rose?

Wouldn't it be more practical to get her a minor appliance or something useful?

The reason one person gives another a bouquet of roses is that this gift is a way of honoring the other person. It is a way of communicating value and paying homage. It is this kind of extravagance that cries out, "I love you!" A heart of love longs for the opportunity to pay honor.

LIFE APPLICATION | Heart Check

We all need to check our hearts when it comes to the matter of giving. Do we have hearts that are overflowing in response to God's goodness, or has the well run dry? When was the last time you found yourself looking for ways to give toward God's work? When was the last time a pastor stood up in your church and said, "Attention, members of the congregation, please stop giving! The bills are paid, our missionaries are taken care of, the mortgage has been burned, all salaries are paid, and we simply have too much. No more offerings until we find a way to spend what we have saved from all your generous gifts."

ILLUSTRATION | The Middle of Life

The placement of the tabernacle gives a visual picture of how God wants to be in the very center of our lives. God had his people arrange their lives, physically and spiritually, around the tabernacle. When they set up camp, the tent of meeting was to be in the very center. Then the priests camped around the tent. Finally, all the tribes of Israel camped surrounding the tabernacle. There were to be three tribes on the north, three on the south, three on the east, and three on the west.

CREATIVE MESSAGE IDEA | A Picture of God's Presence

Show the congregation a picture of how the tabernacle was central in the community of God's people. Have a flip chart and draw the tabernacle, then the tents of the priests, and finally the tribes of Israel all around the tabernacle. Let this visual picture help people see that God was central among his people.

You Will Need:
- A flip chart
- Wide-tip markers

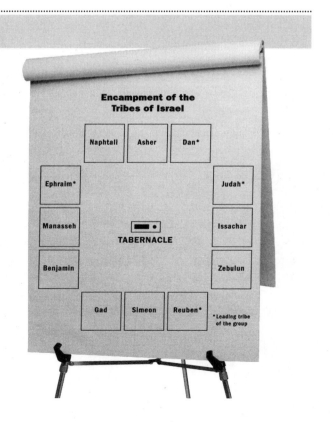

Encampment of the Tribes of Israel

Naphtali   Asher   Dan*

Ephraim*   Judah*

Manasseh   TABERNACLE   Issachar

Benjamin   Zebulun

Gad   Simeon   Reuben*

*Leading tribe of the group

The door of each tent was to be facing the tabernacle. The entire community was built around the tabernacle, which represented God's presence in their midst. When they marched, the pieces of the tabernacle were carried in the middle of the congregation. This was a way of physically picturing that they were to be a community centered on God.

NARRATIVE ON LIFE | On the Road

The presence of the tabernacle in the middle of the camp was to serve as an ever-present reminder that God was with his people. This spiritual reality should have a transforming impact on how God's people live.

Here is a modern-day example of how this works. Have you ever noticed how people drive differently when they see a police car near? Traffic can be flying along, and all of a sudden brake lights begin to flash. Everyone slows down. What's going on? A police car has been sighted. The presence of this car reminds people that there is a speed limit and it would be wise to follow it.

The tabernacle had this same kind of impact on the people. When they saw it, they were reminded that God was with them, leading, guiding, and watching. This impacted the way they related to each other and to God.

LIFE APPLICATION | What If?

What if God were watching me in the work place? What if he were present on my school campus? What if God knew what was happening behind closed doors? What if God were with me every moment of every day?

The tabernacle reminds us that God *is* with us all the time. Through his Holy Spirit he is still present. We need to live each moment with a clear awareness that God is with us, that he still tabernacles among his people. This should have a powerful impact on all we do.

INTERPRETIVE INSIGHT | The House of God

The tabernacle was to be the "dwelling place" of God (Leviticus 26:11). It is important to note that the tabernacle and its furnishings were built along the lines of an ancient Near Eastern home. If you could have visited the home of a Near Eastern nomad at that time, you would have noticed that the structure of the average dwelling place was similar to the tabernacle. The objects that were placed in the tabernacle would also have been found in most homes in that day. They would have been made of more common materials, but the basic concept was the same.

The tabernacle had a large outer courtyard that was 75 feet wide and 150 feet long—about half the length of a football field and not as wide. This outer courtyard was enclosed by a structure with wooden frames and brilliant curtains so that it could be torn down and transported. Much like a fenced-in yard in our day, these frames and curtains offered a kind of safe, quiet place for people to gather and meet with God.

2. The Furnishing in the Tabernacle

INTERPRETIVE INSIGHT | The Bronze Altar

SIGNIFICANT SCRIPTURE

Exodus 25; 27:1-8; 28:29; 30:1-10; Romans 12:1

As a person entered the courtyard of the tabernacle, the first object to be noticed would be the altar. In homes in those days there was generally some kind of grill or pit for cooking food. In the tabernacle the bronze altar for sacrifices was the equivalent of the grill in a home. This altar is described in Exodus 27:1–8. The bronze altar was about 7 -1/2 feet square and about 4 -1/2 feet high. There were horns on each side, and animals would be tied to the horns and offered as a sacrifice.

The burnt offering. Sometimes people think that back in those days, animal sacrifices happened all over Israel on a regular basis. As a general rule, sacrifices only happened in the tabernacle. There were five main types of sacrifices, and it is important that we have a basic sense of what they were.

One offering was called the burnt offering. This offering was distinct because the entire animal was consumed by the fire. Most of the other sacrifices were actually part of a meal. A person or the family would go to the tabernacle, and priests would literally butcher the meat and bring it back to the person or family who offered it, and they would have a meal as a part of worship.

But the burnt offering didn't work that way. In the burnt offering, the whole animal was consumed by fire. Nobody could eat any part of it. All of it was offered to God, and it was a picture of total consecration. As the people saw the offering being consumed, they were reminded that Israel was to be *totally devoted* to God.

The grain offering. The grain offering was designated for the poor who couldn't afford an animal for the burnt offering. A lot of people fell into that category. The beauty of this offering or sacrifice was that it revealed the heart of God for all people. God's sacrificial system was designed to teach that everybody—no matter how rich or how poor—has something to offer God.

The fellowship (peace) offering. Peace or fellowship offerings were offered as expressions of intimacy to God. When somebody had received an unexpected blessing, they would bring a fellowship offering to honor God for his goodness. This sacrifice was a tangible way to say thank you to God. At other times someone would make a vow or commitment of something they wanted to do for God. This offering would be a way of declaring that they were serious about their commitment. At other times when somebody just wanted to say, "God, I love you," they would bring what was called a freewill offering. This was another kind of peace offering.

The sin and guilt offerings. There were two other kinds of offerings called sin offerings and guilt offerings. They were very closely related. They were offered as expressions of sorrow or repentance for wrongdoing. When someone was aware of personal sin, he or she would give an offering. When they were dealing with guilt and wanted to express sorrow to God, they brought an offering. These offerings were important in the process of atonement. Guilt offerings often involved an act that required financial restitution if they had wronged someone.

The entire sacrificial system, which was detailed and complex, pointed forward to a final sacrifice that would be offered for sins. One day Jesus would come and would become the perfect sacrifice. Until then, the sacrificial system reminded people of the cost of sin and the hope of cleansing and restored relationship with God.

LIFE APPLICATION | My Sacrifice

There are many ways we can offer ourselves as living sacrifices. We can offer up a sacrifice of thanksgiving and praise as we cry out, "Thank you." We can offer our hearts in confession as we say, "I want to confess my sin and my sorrow to you. Cleanse me and change my heart and life." We can offer up surrendered lives as we pray, "God, I'll obey you even if it's painful. I will stay on the altar and let you do what you will with my life." The altar may not be sitting in the entrance area of the tabernacle, but it still exists, and we are called to lay down our lives on it every day!

....

There is but one king that I know;
It is he that I love and worship.
If I were to be killed a thousand times for my loyalty to him,
I would still be his servant.
Christ is on my lips,
Christ is in my heart;
No amount of suffering will take him from me.

GENESIUS OF ROME (MARTYR, THIRD CENTURY)

NEW TESTAMENT CONNECTION
Living Sacrifices

The above-mentioned sacrifices took place every day. They were offered first thing in the morning and last thing in the evening. The priests would offer sacrifices for individuals, for families, and for the nation. This altar is the picture the apostle Paul has in mind in Romans 12:1 when he writes, "Offer your bodies as living sacrifices."

The picture would have been clear in the minds of the Jews. When an animal was to be sacrificed, it was tied to the horns that were on the corners of the altar. It didn't have the option to say, "Well, I think I'm done now. I'm going to get up and leave." It was tied to the altar, and there was no way off the altar except through death. Paul's words in Romans 12 are an expression of utter surrender and submission. Like the animal tied to the altar, we are bound to give our whole lives in sacrifice to the God who sacrificed all for us.

INTERPRETIVE INSIGHT | The Basin

The next thing someone would see upon entering the courtyard of the tabernacle was a large bronze basin. In it the priests cleansed themselves before and after washing the sacrifice. The basin was a common amenity in ancient Near Eastern homes. People entering homes were dusty and dirty and felt a need to clean up. We live in such a clean society that we can't imagine what it would be like to be dirty most of the time. But in those days, when a person entered a dwelling, there was usually a basin for cleansing. In the tabernacle, therefore, there was a similar piece of furniture—the basin.

INTERPRETIVE INSIGHT | A Clear Conscience

In Bible times people didn't have the opportunity to get cleaned up very often. When they did, it was an act of gracious hospitality. In the tabernacle a large part of what the priests did was to butcher animals. That's a messy job. In Exodus 30:17 we learn that the basin was placed between the altar and the Tent of Meeting so that when the priests entered God's presence, they could clean themselves first "so that they will not die" (Exodus 30:20).

This is a picture of being clean in the sight of God and what that means. Such cleansing was not just for the body, not just for the clothes, but especially for the conscience. Through this symbolism, people realized that God offered purity. Imagine a heart with no stain, no regret, and no remorse.

LIFE APPLICATION | Cleanse Me, Lord

We live in a world that is unclean. We can feel the grit and grime of the world cling to our minds and souls. Yet God still offers cleansing. God offers purity of heart, even for the greatest of sinners. As we look into the water of the bronze basin, we see a reflection—ourselves. We see our sin, our offenses, our hopelessness. But as we plunge beneath the water, we are reminded that God has the power to cleanse. Jesus has offered to make us white as snow, if we will receive his cleansing.

INTERPRETIVE INSIGHT | The Holy Place (Outer Chamber)

Inside the tabernacle proper was an outer chamber called the Holy Place. In an ancient Near Eastern home, there was a place where you could receive a guest and perhaps break bread. In the tabernacle there were three main pieces of furniture in the Holy Place, similar to common furnishings in homes at that time: a lampstand, burning incense, and fresh bread.

INTERPRETIVE INSIGHT | The Lampstand

The lampstand is described in Exodus 25:31. It was made of pure hammered gold, and the priest's job was to keep it filled with olive oil so that the flame would never go out. It remained lit all through the night.

Why did they do this? This is the one part of the tabernacle that could be seen from the outside. The ever-burning light was a little bit like leaving a porch light on to send a message that somebody's home. Anybody in Israel could come to the courtyard, even at night, when they were alone, when they were worried, and there was a light on in God's house. Somebody was home!

ILLUSTRATION | Leave the Light On

In a popular commercial for the motel chain called Motel 6, the spokesperson would always end by saying the same line, "We'll leave the light on for you." The advertising hook was to make possible customers feel they are always welcome. In the same way, God said to his priests, "Don't let the lamp go out. I want all my people to know that when they're confused, when they're afraid, when they're in the dark, I'll leave the light on. I am here. I am available to them all day and all night."

LIFE APPLICATION | Walking in the Light

Some of those who gather to hear this message will be living in dark times. They may wonder if God is really there or if they are welcome to enter his presence. They need to know that God has a light burning for them. Remind them of God's light that never goes out. Remind them that God cares so much that his light burns twenty-four hours a day, seven days a week, three hundred and sixty-five days a year. We can enter his presence any time. We don't have to wait until tomorrow. God is available now!

INTERPRETIVE INSIGHT | The Altar of Incense

When you entered the Holy Place, you would see the altar of incense (see the description in Exodus 30:1–10). In homes in the ancient Near East at this time in history, people often burned incense to cover up the odor of people who did not bathe often, animals that lived in the house, and the smell of animals that had been slaughtered and cooked for family meals. The tabernacle had incense burning in the entry area of the Holy Place. This would have been a relief, since the smell of slaughtered animals would have been intense throughout the entire tabernacle.

> **NEW TESTAMENT CONNECTION**
>
> ## The Prayers of God's People
>
> In Revelation 5:8 we read about the golden bowls full of incense. We are told these are the prayers of the saints, a sweet thing to God. Incense is a picture of a sweet aroma ascending to God. As God's people, we must learn that our prayers are sweet to God and that they ascend like fragrant incense.

INTERPRETIVE INSIGHT | The Bread of the Presence

In the Holy Place was also the table of the Presence. It was built of wood and covered with gold. The serving utensils also were made of gold. The primary purpose of this table was to hold the bread of the Presence. Every week the priests were to bake twelve loaves of bread, one for each of the twelve tribes of Israel.

ILLUSTRATION | The Smell of Freshly Baked Bread

Have you ever smelled freshly baked bread? It is one of the most powerful aromas! If you walk into a home and are met by the smell of freshly baked bread, something happens. A feeling of warmth comes over you. A smile finds its way to your lips. You might even begin to salivate a little, as your mouth and body imagine partaking of this simple but wonderful delicacy. This is true today if we visit the home of a friend and smell freshly baked bread, and it was true when priests came into the Holy Place and smelled the fresh baked bread of the Presence.

LIFE APPLICATION | Seeing the Face of God

One of the reasons the bread was called "the bread of the Presence" is that it pointed to the warm, fresh, sweet presence of God. Literally, the expression means "the bread of the face." This was the bread that was always before the face of God. It was also bread that reminded the Israelites of the face of God through his daily provision and fresh presence every day.

God is still present today. He shows himself in new and fresh ways. He provides our daily bread and all we need. What we need to do is learn to see his face. We need to look and see the face of God's presence in each loaf of bread, each meal, each friendship, each paycheck, and each gentle breeze of the Holy

HISTORICAL CONTEXT | Table Fellowship

Breaking bread and sharing table fellowship (a meal) with others was important in Bible times. In our day, we tend to sit down for a meal only with people we know and like. But in those days there was deep meaning in sharing a meal and breaking bread. When you broke bread, you were entering a level of intimate fellowship that was much deeper than what we express through a shared meal in our culture today.

This is why the religious leaders of Jesus' day were so outraged when Jesus, a rabbi, actually broke bread with sinners. He was entering an intimate experience with people who were to be avoided, according to the religious laws of the day. In the days of Moses, everyone knew that breaking bread and sharing table fellowship was a sign of deep intimacy. With that in mind, the idea that God would have bread prepared for his people spoke volumes about God's desire to be close to his people.

Sprit that blows into our lives. We need to learn to see, taste, feel, hear, and even smell the presence of God!

INTERPRETIVE INSIGHT | The Most Holy Place (Holy of Holies)

After passing through the Holy Place, seeing the light, and smelling the bread, the priests encountered a heavy veil, a blue, purple, and scarlet curtain. These were rich, majestic colors. This curtain was the entrance to the Most Holy Place (the Holy of Holies). This was the room of greatest intimacy, much as a bedroom would be in a home. It was set aside for only the most intimate companion of God, the high priest. Access to it was restricted to once a year.

INTERPRETIVE INSIGHT | The Ark of the Testimony

Exodus 25 tells us about the single piece of furnishing in the Most Holy Place: "the ark of the Testimony [covenant]." It was a place where atonement could be made for the sins of the people. This ark was a box made of acacia wood and overlaid with gold—forty-five inches long, about twenty-seven inches high, and twenty-seven inches wide.

God said regarding the ark: "I want you to put poles on that ark so it cannot be touched, because it's holy. It's set apart." Here are God's instructions about the formation of the ark:

> Make an atonement cover of pure gold—two and a half cubits long and a cubit and a half wide. And make two cherubim out of hammered gold at the ends of the cover. Make one cherub on one end and the second cherub on the other; make the cherubim of one piece with the cover, at the two ends. The cherubim are to have their wings spread upward, overshadowing the cover with them. The cherubim are to face each other, looking toward the cover. (Exodus 25:17–20)

HISTORICAL CONTEXT | One Penalty

There was one specific penalty prescribed for anyone who entered the Most Holy Place without being invited: death! Now, this might seem extreme and excessive, but this was a place of unsurpassed intimacy. You did not just barge into the Most Holy Place. As a matter of fact, only the high priest entered this place, and he only went in once a year!

It is interesting to note that there was also a prescribed penalty for violating the bed chamber in the home of a family in Israel. If a person invaded the bedroom and committed adultery, the penalty was death. There was this similar penalty because adultery involved breaking the most intimate boundary in the home.

People often wonder what these cherubs looked like. Today we tend to think of cherubs as cute, chubby little valentine figures. But that's not accurate at all. These were mighty angelic beings of great power. But even these great forces in the universe humble themselves before the awesome presence of God. They bow down!

In Exodus 25:22 God says, "There, above the cover between the two cherubim that are over the ark of the Testimony, I will meet with you and give you all my commands for the Israelites." It is as if God is saying, "I'll come sit on a box in a tent, and you'll know I'm always with you. I will guide you." What an amazing picture of God's willingness to be present with his people, right where they are.

3. Entering God's Presence with Confidence

Interpretive Insight: What's in the Box?

One way God invited his people to come near to him was through simple reminders. In the ark, God had the people place some objects that would always be there to help them see that they are welcome to come near to him.

The first object was a bowl of manna. This was a reminder that God would always be faithful and provide, one day at a time.

Next was Aaron's rod. The people knew the story (from Numbers 17) about how God miraculously caused Aaron's rod to bud as an expression to all the Israelites that God had chosen Aaron and his descendents to be priests to lead them in worship. This second object was a reminder that God invites his people to come near and worship.

Finally, God told the people to put the two tablets that contained the Ten Commandments into the box. This was the people's copy and God's copy of the covenant. It was God's reminder that they were to draw near to him with obedient hearts.

Each item in the box taught a lesson and gave a reminder from God for his people:

- Manna—trust me.

- The rod of Aaron—worship me.

- The tablets of the Ten Commandments—obey me.

Trust, worship, and obedience represent the heart of what it means to live with God. The objects in the box became symbols and reminders of God's desire for intimacy with his people.

LIFE APPLICATION | Life with God

The entire tabernacle, beginning with the altar, ending with the ark of the covenant, and everything in between, was an invitation to draw near to God. This place was a visible sign that God had open arms extended to his people.

God still has arms open to us today. We need to notice the reminders all around us. God still provides for us—each meal, each paycheck, and each breath of life is a reminder of his love. God still meets us in worship; when we feel his presence and the moving of the Holy Spirit, we are reminded that his arms are open. God's law still leads and guides our lives; we need to hear him speak through his Word. God's invitation for us to draw near to him is being extended over and over, every day.

> *To those who are tried by the tempest,*
> *You are the calm harbor;*
> *You are the object of all that hope.*
> *To those who are sick, you are health;*
> *You guide the blind and give help to those in need.*
> *To those who face suffering, you always grant mercy,*
> *You are a light in darkness, a place of rest for the weary.*
>
> SEVERUS OF THRACE (THIRD CENTURY)

INTERPRETIVE INSIGHT | The Ephod

Skilled workers fashioned an ephod, a kind of vest with twelve precious stones, for the high priest. This article of clothing had powerful symbolism. Each one of the stones was to have the name of one of the twelve tribes of Israel on it. Exodus 28:29 says, "Whenever Aaron enters the Holy Place, he will bear the names of the sons of Israel over his heart on the breastpiece of decision as a continuing memorial before the LORD." He was to carry all of the people on his heart every time he came before the Lord. This is a beautiful picture of what a priest was to do—carry the people on his heart to God.

INTERPRETIVE INSIGHT | The Leading of the Holy Spirit

The priests had something called the Urim and Thummim. These were concrete, tangible objects designed to train the priests to consult God, to pray, to listen, and to submit before making a major decision. There is a lot of speculation as to what they were, but we can be certain they were tools God used to teach them to seek his will in every decision.

NEW TESTAMENT CONNECTION
A Holy Priesthood

In 1 Peter 2:9 we read: "But you are a chosen people, a royal priesthood, a holy nation, a people belonging to God, that you may declare the praises of him who called you out of darkness into his wonderful light." Today, every person who is a follower of Jesus is one of his royal priests.

In other words, since the coming of Christ and the sending of the Holy Spirit, we are a priesthood of believers. There are many acts of ministry that we can enter into as God's priests, but here are a few practical areas we can all see to move into priestly ministry: (1) We can declare praises to God. As Peter teaches us, this is a responsibility of a priest. (2) We can lift up others in prayer, interceding on behalf of those in the family of God. Our prayers are part of a priestly ministry. (3) We can carry the names of God's people on our hearts. We might not have a literal ephod to wear, but we can inscribe the names of God's people into our hearts and seek to love them in the name of God.

Too often we do dumb things and make foolish decisions because we don't seek God's guidance. The priests of God were trained to seek God and to pray for wisdom. Like them, we too can seek God and ask for wisdom. We must pray with confidence that God can still give specific guidance to us. He is perfectly capable and willing to guide us through the Holy Spirit. God calls us to slow down and listen. He wants us to search his Word closely and follow his leading.

NARRATIVE ON THE TEXT | A Day of Cleansing

Leviticus 16 records the events of the Day of Atonement. This was a day for cleansing from sin—a time of new beginnings. On this day the whole community came to a stop. Nobody worked. Nobody ate. On this day alone, the Most Holy Place was entered. This was a way of teaching the people that their sins were keeping them from intimacy with God.

Imagine the people of Israel gathered around the courtyard; everybody is watching. Then Aaron, the high priest, begins to offer a sacrifice to atone for his own sin, because he is a sinner just like everybody else.

Next, he prepares to make a sacrifice for all the people. Aaron, the high priest, takes the blood from that sacrifice and goes into the Most Holy Place to sprinkle the blood on the atonement cover on the ark of the covenant. While Aaron is in the Most Holy Place, all the people stand outside waiting. Some of them are praying. Some of them are crying. Some of them are explaining to their children what's happening. All of them are deeply aware of the reason Aaron is in the Most Holy Place. They are sinners, and he is there to deal with their sins. On this day, everybody remembers their sin.

The crowd is filled with people like you and me: greedy people who have cheated others, people whose marriages are falling apart, people who struggle with sexual sin, parents who have short tempers with their children, people with every sin imaginable; they all stand there and wait.

Will the priest come back out soon? Is everything alright? Will God show up? Is God still with them even though they struggle with sin? Can they truly be forgiven? These and countless other questions are swirling through their minds.

There was an ancient teaching that the high priest was not to remain too long in the Most Holy Place lest he put Israel in terror. As the people wait, the tension mounts. Then, finally, he came out. The people search his face for any expression; they watch his every move.

Next the high priest takes another animal, a goat, chosen by lot, and places his hands on the goat's head and confesses the sins of all the people. This goes on for some time. As Aaron does this, the people think of all their sins and know that in some way Aaron's hands on this animal have to do with them and their sins. Then, as Leviticus 16:22 tells us, the goat is sent away: "The goat will carry on itself all their sins to a solitary place; and the man shall release it in the desert."

Finally, the people can breathe again. All is well. They have been reminded of their forgiveness for another year. Year after year and decade after decade pass by as over and over again the high priest goes through the same process. Generations of people are born, live, sin, confess, and die. In all of this God is teaching his people about his presence.

NEW TESTAMENT CONNECTION | ## The Lamb of God

The tabernacle was the beginning of God's teaching about the coming of Jesus, Immanuel, God with us. In the gospel of John we read, "In the beginning was the Word, and the Word was with God, and the Word was God" (John 1:1). Later in the same chapter we discover that this Word is Jesus, God in human flesh, "The Word became flesh and made his dwelling among us. We have seen his glory, the glory of the One and Only, who came from the Father, full of grace and truth" (John 1:14).

Any Jewish person in the first century would have recognized the word for "made his dwelling among us" as the word that meant Jesus "camped," "tented," or "tabernacled" with us. The Greek word meant "to tabernacle." When any Jewish person read these words in John's gospel, they saw an immediate connection to the glory and presence of God as experienced in the wilderness tabernacle.

Another New Testament connection with the tabernacle is found in Hebrews 9–10. These two chapters are all about the tabernacle. They reflect on how the tabernacle has been fulfilled by what Jesus did. In Hebrews 10:19–22 we read:

> Therefore, brothers, since we have confidence to enter the Most Holy Place by the blood of Jesus, by a new and living way opened for us through the curtain, that is, his body, and since we have a great priest over the house of God, let us draw near to God with a sincere heart in full assurance of faith, having our hearts sprinkled to cleanse us from a guilty conscience and having our bodies washed with pure water.

We can now enter the Most Holy Place with confidence because of Jesus. Once again God is dwelling with his people. But this time, everyone can have access.

Note too that when Jesus went to the cross and died for our sins, the veil in the tabernacle was torn in two, and the way to the Most Holy Place was opened for all (Matthew 27:51; Mark 15:38).

Narrowing the Focus

The narrowing of a place. All throughout the building of the tabernacle in the Old Testament, there is a narrowing of focus about God's presence. God says, in effect, "Out of the *whole world* I'm going to come to *one camp,* and I'll come to *one courtyard,* and I'll come to *one tent,* and I'll come to *one box,* and that will be the place where I dwell."

The narrowing of a people. God says, "Out of *all the people* on earth, I'll come to *one nation,* I'll come to *one tribe*—the tribe of Levi. I'll come to a subset of that tribe, *the priests*—Aaron and his descendents. And I'll come to *one man,* to the high priest."

The narrowing of a time. God also says, "Out of the *year* I will choose *one month,* the tenth month. Out of this month I will choose *one week, one day,* and finally, *one moment.*" That moment was when the high priest laid his hands on the head of the goat. Similarly, at one climactic moment, Jesus became the final sacrifice for sins.

God says, "One place, one man, one moment; I'll be there." The tabernacle taught people for centuries. It pointed forward to the day of Jesus. Then God said, "Now the Word has become flesh; and the Word has tabernacled among us. We saw his glory, and we saw it most fully on the cross." At that one moment the veil was ripped in two, and the greatest invitation in all human history was extended: Come to God; the way is open.

God's Dwelling Place

Where is the Most Holy Place today? It is here and now! Any place can be the dwelling of God. Anybody is welcome to come. Any time is fine! In Christ there was a shift in the fabric of eternity from one place, one man, and one moment to the reality in which we live—anybody, anytime, anywhere.

Where is the Most Holy Place? It could be in your living room. It could be at your desk at work tomorrow. It could be on your construction site or on your high school campus. The God who was present in Israel's Most Holy Place can be present in all of his glory as you drive in your car. Right here, right now, you can tabernacle with God!

**CREATIVE
MESSAGE IDEA**

Meeting God at the Table

This message could lead very naturally into a communion experience. You may want to close your service by sharing together in the Lord's Supper.

Loving God's Law

THE BOOK OF DEUTERONOMY

The Heart of the
MESSAGE

Jesus said, "For where your treasure is, there your heart will be also" (Matthew 6:21). We live in a world that invites us to fall in love with something new every day. New products, new hobbies, new culinary sensations, and new entertainments cry out for our attention. Yet, in the midst of this cacophony of voices, God speaks to us and invites us to love his law. God does not scream his invitation; he simply sets before us the richness of his law and invites us to hear, learn, and grow to cherish the words of life and truth that his people have loved for millennia.

This message gives a window into the heart of the law as expressed in the book of Deuteronomy. When we get a clear picture of what God's law truly teaches, we begin to see why it was the prized possession of the nation of Israel. When we taste the goodness of God's law, we start to hunger for more. As we meet God, the Lawgiver, we fall more in love with him and his law.

The Heart of the
MESSENGER

Do you love God's law? Do you meditate on it day and night? Do you find yourself hungering to know God's law in deeper ways? As you prepare to bring this message, meditate on the goodness of God's law. Consider taking time each day of the coming week to read a section of Psalm 119. This psalm celebrates God's law in a way that will draw you in and invite you to see it in new and fresh ways. As you read, reflect on the following questions:

> When was a time that I really fell deeper in love with God's Word?

> What life experiences draw me deeper into God's Word?

> What can I do to make the personal study of Scripture a bigger priority in my life?

**Brief Message
OUTLINE**

1 Laws regarding giving and generosity

2 Laws regarding feasts and celebrations

3 "Head-scratching" laws

Introduction: Loving the Law

Deuteronomy is quoted more than eighty times in the New Testament. Only Genesis, Isaiah, and the Psalms are quoted this often. It's a very influential and powerful book that turns our heart to the law of God. In Deuteronomy we discover that God sees his people, he knows his people, and he is committed to transform them into a nation that honors him and reflects his righteous heart in a world that is dark and sin-filled. This same God still wants his children to be transformed through the process of growing in knowledge and love of his law.

INTERPRETIVE INSIGHT | A Beginning and an End

Imagine the setting for a moment. The people of Israel are about to enter the Promised Land after forty years of waiting. They're excited, they're afraid, they're overwhelmed, and they're curious. But Moses is not going with them. For forty years they've relied on him for all of their spiritual leadership, and now they will be moving forward without him.

For them this is just the start of their adventure, but for Moses this is the end. Moses is going to die. He knows it and they know it. This is a poignant moment in their history. What we read in Deuteronomy are the last words Moses will say to this group of people whom he has led, helped to liberate, struggled with, wrestled with, yelled at, and loved for forty years.

Deuteronomy is structured as the final message that Moses gives to these people. It comes in three sessions, or three talks. What is interesting is that Moses does not do what most people do at retirement events. He does not reminisce about his career or all he has accomplished in his life. Rather, by the inspiration of the Holy Spirit, he gives one more appeal to the people of Israel. He calls them to follow God's plan, God's law for their lives.

HISTORICAL CONTEXT | The Cost of a Stubborn Heart!

In the opening two verses of Deuteronomy we get a brief geography lesson. We are told that "it takes *eleven days* to go from Horeb to Kadesh Barnea by the Mount Seir road."

This information might seem a little random at first, but it is there for a specific reason. This is not just bonus information on travel times on an ancient road. The writer wants every reader to remember that the trip from Mount Sinai, which is also known as Horeb, up to the edge of the Promised Land, *normally* takes only eleven days.

Thus, a trip that usually took a week and a half took Israel forty years to complete. The writer of Deuteronomy is subtly setting the context here: A whole generation of human beings wasted their lives in the desert and lost the opportunity to enter God's Promised Land because of their stubborn refusal to trust God and do what he said. The writer is also saying to all future readers, including us, "Don't make the same mistake. Don't blow forty years of your life on an eleven-day lesson."

In the first three chapters, Moses reviews what God has done and how often the people stumbled and messed up. Then he gives this appeal (Deuteronomy 4:1–2):

> Hear now, O Israel, the decrees and laws I am about to teach you. Follow them so that you may live and may go in and take possession of the land that the LORD, the God of your fathers, is giving you. Do not add to what I command you and do not subtract from it, but keep the commands of the LORD your God that I give you.

INTERPRETIVE INSIGHT | ## A Prized Possession

The law was Israel's prized possession. In Deuteronomy 4:5–14 we see that the laws of God were to be followed in a way that the world would look on in amazement. God's people knew that following the law would make them wise and discerning. They also knew that the world would look at them and see God's presence and power as they walked in obedience to his laws.

Moses calls the people to reflect deeply on this question: "What other nation is so great as to have such righteous decrees and laws as this body of laws I am setting before you today?" (Deuteronomy 4:8). Their military force, wealth, or position in the eyes of the world did not establish their greatness. Their prized possession was not the tabernacle, Solomon's temple, or even the Promised Land once they entered. The people of Israel identified the law of God as the one thing that set them apart among the nations. It was their most valued treasure.

God's law was so prized that the people were to keep their eyes focused on it. They were to hold tightly to his teachings so they would not slip through their fingers, out of their hearts, and be lost. This is an interesting image in light of the fact that later in their history, the people of Israel lost their focus, let their grasp on the law slip, and actually lost it. Recall that in the days of King Josiah, as the temple was being renovated, a copy of the law was rediscovered (2 Kings 22:1–13). Its contents shocked the king, since he was unaware of what it said.

WORD STUDY

The Second Telling of the Law

Deuteronomy is a desperate plea for people to *remember* and *follow* God's law. The name Deuteronomy comes from two Greek words:

- *deuteros*, meaning "second"
- *nomos*, meaning "law"

In other words this book is a second telling or second giving of the law. God knows we all need reminders, and Moses brings the people of God back to the truth they have already heard but need to hear again.

LIFE APPLICATION | Remembering God's Law

In Deuteronomy 6:4–8 we see that God's intent is clear. He wants us to remember his law, and not for just a moment. It is for the next generation, and for those who follow after them. God does not want us to remember his law in the way that a high school student crams for an exam and then forgets everything after the test is done. He wants his law so deep in our hearts that nothing can shake it loose.

The picture God paints for us in Deuteronomy is vivid. Teach his law to the next generation and talk about it throughout the day . . . any time. Reflect on it and celebrate it everywhere we go. Do whatever it takes to remember God's law. If we need to tie a string around our finger, do it. We can write it on the back of our hand if that's what it takes. Put a Post-It Note on the doorway, on the mirror in the bathroom, on the refrigerator, or anywhere else we might see it. For those who are into technology, they can load it into their hand-held computer, set a reminder alarm throughout the day, and have significant Scriptures pop up just to remind them to meditate on God's law.

INTERPRETIVE INSIGHT | Loving the Law

The people of Israel did not see the law of God as some whip-cracking taskmaster that ruled over them. They loved the law of God. They saw how it was lifting them out of the chaotic darkness of sin and closer to the heart of God. To get a sense of how the people cherished the law, read these verses:

> [The ordinances of the LORD] are more precious than gold,
>   than much pure gold;
> they are sweeter than honey,
>   than honey from the comb. (Psalm 19:10)
>
> Oh, how I love your law!
>   I meditate on it all day long. (Psalm 119:97)
>
> Your statutes are my heritage forever;
>   they are the joy of my heart. (Psalm 119:111)

The wisest people who lived in Israel loved the law with all their hearts. We don't think about the law that much in our day. We certainly don't love and cherish it. It is unlikely that many people meditate on the legal code of their city or state. We don't love our law that way. But the Israelites saw their law as the greatest source of wisdom the world had ever seen.

1. Laws Regarding Giving and Generosity

One of the first words most children learn to say is, "Mine!" By nature we are selfish and seek our own good. Yet God is committed to help us learn the joy of generosity. He wants us to see that giving and sharing are part of his plan for our maturity. The book of Deuteronomy is filled with instruction on how God's people are called to grow in a spirit of giving. As we study Deuteronomy, we will discover that God still calls his children to a life of generosity that grows out of a profound understanding that God has given us more than we can imagine or dream.

NARRATIVE ON THE TEXT | God's Call to Giving

The tithe—10 percent. Leviticus 27:30 says, "A tithe of everything from the land, whether grain from the soil or fruit from the trees, belongs to the LORD; it is holy to the LORD." It is common knowledge in the church that followers of Christ are still called to give the first 10 percent of their income (harvest) to God. This was true back then and it is still true now.

SIGNIFICANT SCRIPTURE

Deuteronomy 15:1–8;
24:19–22;
Leviticus 27:30; 25:2, 8–12

CREATIVE MESSAGE IDEA | You Do the Math

Use a flip chart as you walk through the various Old Testament laws about giving and generosity. Each time you finish a category, write the percentage on the board. Use this as a visual aid to help people see that the people of Israel were called to a level of sacrificial giving that would stretch most Christ-followers today.

As you begin this exercise, do two things. First, ask people to take out a piece of paper and a pen or pencil. Invite them to follow along with you. Next, ask them to write down their guess as to what percentage of his or her income a faithful Israelite would give to God if he or she simply followed the teaching in the law. When you are done, your chart will look like this:

Tithe 10%
Sabbath Year 14%
Jubilee Year 2%
Gleaning Laws 4%
(estimate)
_____
TOTAL 30%

The Sabbath year—14 percent. The giving for a faithful Israelite didn't stop with the tithe. In Leviticus 25:2 we read about what was called a Sabbath year. Out of concern for the earth that God had made, God says, "Every seventh year, people are not to plant anything. No sowing, no reaping, let the land rest."

That meant they would give up their income and produce a seventh of the time. Moreover, Deuteronomy 15:1 taught the people to cancel debts on the Sabbath year. The people were to forget debts and celebrate God's goodness and provision. This meant that the people of Israel would give up 14 percent of their income because, in an agricultural economy, these commands meant they would have no income for a full year every seven years!

ILLUSTRATION | A Call You Will Never Get

Try to imagine this Sabbath spirit in our world today. You are sitting at home one evening doing your bills. You feel tension because the pile of bills is getting larger and your income is not. You are looking at the balance in your checkbook, trying to figure out how you can make ends meet for this month. All of a sudden the phone rings and startles you. You pick it up and swallow hard when you realize it is a representative from your credit card company.

You begin to explain to them that you were just sitting down to do your bills and that the check will be in the mail by the morning. They tell you not to send a check. You worry that this is some kind of a threat and that maybe they are sending over a collection agent to "make you pay." At this point they explain that it is the seventh year since you opened your account with them, so they are going to wipe your account clean. You have a zero balance! You owe them nothing. The debt and all interest are gone.

Can you imagine this happening? Of course not—and it won't. But it did happen back in Moses' day. The people following God's law learned how to live with this level of generosity.

NARRATIVE ON THE TEXT | God's Call to Giving (continued)

Jubilee year—2 percent. For a faithful Israelite, the giving did not stop there. Leviticus 25:8–12 teaches us that every forty-nine years God declared a year of Jubilee. Like the Sabbath year, it was a time when the earth rested and there was no planting or harvesting. It was also a time when debts were forgiven and people were set free from bondage.

This is a great picture in the Old Testament. When Jesus came, he used Jubilee language to describe the era he inaugurated. It would be a time when freedom came for all people. To prevent chronic poverty, God said in effect, "Every fifty years, all the land is to go back to its original owner." This was a radical redistribution of the wealth, where everyone got back the family inheritance that had been established in the time of Joshua.

There were two Jubilee years in every century. This meant that the Israelites would lose a full percent of income if they observed the two Jubilee years. In practical terms, this meant the giving of 2 percent of their income to the Lord.

Gleaning laws—4–5 percent. It would seem that Israelites who gave their tithes, observed the Sabbath years, and also celebrated the year of Jubilee, would be doing enough. Think about it, this is 26 percent of their income. But God was calling them to radical and sacrificial generosity. Deuteronomy 24:19–22 says:

> When you are harvesting in your field and you overlook a
> sheaf, do not go back to get it. Leave it for the alien, the
> fatherless and the widow, so that the LORD your God may bless
> you in all the work of your hands. When you beat the olives
> from your trees, do not go over the branches a second time.
> Leave what remains for the alien, the fatherless and the widow.
> When you harvest the grapes in your vineyard, do not go over
> the vines again. Leave what remains for the alien, the fatherless
> and the widow. Remember that you were slaves in Egypt. That is
> why I command you to do this.

God is telling his people to be a little sloppy when they farm. They could have gone over the fields twice and beat the olive trees a little harder to be sure everything fell to the ground, and thus they could have made a bigger profit at the market and gotten a better return on their investment. But God called them to be sloppy and always leave some in their fields.

Why? Because something inside the human heart tends to say, "I've got to wring every ounce of profit out of this I can. I've got to make every dime I can grab." To counteract this selfish tendency, God instituted the gleaning laws. These laws moved God's people to show tender compassion for the poor and needy. They were to leave something in the fields and on the trees so the poor could come through and get a little harvest to help meet their needs. It was a sign of the compassion of God extended through the hands of his people. It's hard to estimate what percentage of income the Israelites would give away from these gleaning practices, but it is safe to say it was at least 4 to 5 percent.

Final conclusions—30 percent or more! What's the total amount that would be given by the child of God who faithfully observed the laws of generosity? Faithful Israelites would give an average of 30 percent of their income to God and those in need. This is a pretty amazing thing. People often think Old Testament law calls people to give only 10 percent. The truth is, an Israelite who was devoutly following the law would have given closer to 30 percent. And it would have been higher if you include freewill offerings, which were common in those days.

ILLUSTRATION | "Mine!" and "Not Mine!"

Outside of the word "no," what's a two-year-old's favorite word in the whole world? It is "Mine!" Just think about it: "My blanket," "my toys," "my food," "mine, mine, mine!" This propensity to be selfish is deep in the heart of human beings. Yet God says, "I want you to learn how to let go. I want you to provide for somebody else. So, as you're farming, as you're walking through life, as you're doing your work, I want you to look at all you have and occasionally say, '"Not mine.'"

NARRATIVE ON LIFE | Radical Commitment

In his book *Dedication and Leadership*, Douglas Hyde tells about the radical sacrifice he had seen prior to his becoming a follower of Jesus. Hyde had been a communist during the 1930s and 1940s but had come to see the truth of the Christian faith. What troubled him, and what he writes about in his book, is how much communists were willing to sacrifice for their cause (which was false) and how little Christians were willing to give up for the sake of Jesus.

Hyde had been a leader in the communist party for over twenty years. During most of this time he worked for the British Communist Party's daily paper, the *London Daily Worker*. He, and many others like him, had taken radical pay cuts to leave their jobs in the marketplace and take posts in the communist party. Hyde writes:

> Some of the workers were earning one-tenth of what had been their salary when they had worked for the "capitalist" press. There were times when, small as our salaries were, these could not be paid at all.
>
> Even when the paper became slightly more prosperous and the staff were technically given the union rate for the job, the sacrifices still continued. We got our packets, opened them and immediately gave eight-fourteenths of their contents to the Party and the paper—before it burned our fingers. Since everyone did this, it became something of a meaningless ritual after a while and so we did not bother even to receive the cash, it just went direct to the cause. And so it continues to this day.

When Hyde came to accept Jesus as the leader of his life, he was staggered by the meager expectations of the church when it came to his finances. He had seen people take a 90-percent pay cut to work for the communist cause. Then these same people (including him for twenty years), who had already given so much, gave over 50 percent of every paycheck to the cause. Now he heard that the church was calling people to give 10 percent to the cause of Christ. He was shocked by the small amount, and even more shocked that so few people responded to this call. Hyde also writes:

> The Communist's appeal to idealism is direct and audacious. They say if you make mean little demands upon people, you will get a mean little response which is all you deserve, but, if you make big demands on them, you will get an historic response.

Hyde writes these things not to praise the Communist Party but to challenge those who follow Christ. If people can follow a misguided cause with such reckless abandon, why can't Christ's followers learn to sacrifice with a joy-filled surrender? Of all people, it is Christians who should be most generous and willing to sacrifice, because our Savior has sacrificed everything for us!

LIFE APPLICATION | Tightfisted or Openhanded?

The goal of the Old Testament laws is never to make us mechanical in our responses. In Deuteronomy 15:7–8 we read, "If there is a poor man among your brothers in any of the towns of the land that the LORD your God is giving you, do not be hardhearted or tightfisted toward your poor brother. Rather be openhanded and freely lend him whatever he needs." Imagine a community where everybody is joyfully openhanded with what they have. Think about what a community of people could be like if they made their resources available to God, to the people of God, and to those in need. We need to ask ourselves how we can grow in generosity and keep our hands open and our resources available.

NARRATIVE ON LIFE | Put It on the Table

At church conferences all over this country, there is a sad reality that restaurant staff members have learned to face. It is simply this: Church leaders and evangelical church members are not always famous for being generous tippers. They are often notorious for being stingier than people who don't even know God. When a leadership conference takes a lunch break and the people flood into the local restaurants (often with their name tags still on), many members of the wait staff brace themselves for the worst.

Yet, it should be just the opposite! Followers of Christ, of all people in the world, should live with an openhanded spirit of giving. We have everything! We are rich in God's mercy and goodness. We should be quick to put a great tip on the table and back it up with a joy-filled attitude.

NEW TESTAMENT CONNECTION

A Dream Comes True

In the book of Acts we see this dream of sacrificial generosity lived out in the early church. The Holy Spirit descended, hearts were changed, and people began to live with an openhanded and giving attitude. "All the believers were together and had everything in common. Selling their possessions and goods, they gave to anyone as he had need" (Acts 2:44–45).

LIFE APPLICATION | Leave Something in the Bag

There are many ways we can apply what we learn from the laws of generosity in Leviticus and Deuteronomy. Most churches or communities have some kind of occasional food drive or a food pantry for those who are in a time of need. One simple discipline is to begin practicing a modern application of the ancient gleaning laws. This might mean committing to buy one or two additional items to give away each time you go to the store. When you get home, put these in a separate bag and set this aside. Once the bag is full, give it away.

This practice will be a simple reminder, every time you go to the store, that God calls you to be generous toward those who are in need. You might even want to call the food pantry and ask them what they most need during that particular season of the year. Many such ministries have changing needs through the year, and being aware of specific needs could help you be strategic in your shopping. Who knows, maybe one day God will prompt you to make a shopping trip and give everything to those who are in need.

Man should not consider his outward possessions as his own, but as common to all, so as to share them without hesitation when others are in need.

THOMAS AQUINAS (THIRTEENTH CENTURY)

2. Laws Regarding Feasts and Celebrations

Too often people see God as solemn and angry. They miss the reality that God is filled with passionate joy and that he calls his children to lives of committed celebration. The book of Deuteronomy recounts God's call for his people to gather for festivals and times of joy-filled remembrance. In Deuteronomy we hear the invitation to live as people who regularly celebrate the goodness of our God.

Right in the middle of Deuteronomy we find laws that have to do with feasting and celebration. There were three main feasts required in the Book of the Law. To help us remember them, we will use analogies from our national (American) experience. If you, as a teacher, are using this teacher's resource but live outside of the United States, you will need to find parallels in your national calendar to use. For instance, in the United States the Passover could be compared to the Fourth of July (Independence Day); in Mexico the best parallel holiday would be Cinco de Mayo.

INTERPRETIVE INSIGHT | Three Great Times of Celebration

Passover (Independence Day). In Deuteronomy 16:1–8 we read about God's call for his people to remember and celebrate their independence from Egypt. The Passover marked their deliverance from bondage and the time they became free as a nation. The Fourth of July is the closest equivalent in the United States to this ancient celebration.

Passover celebrated the time when God's people became independent. But the big difference was that their hero was God. They did not fight for their freedom. Rather, God set them free and then called them to celebrate for a whole week once a year. If you look closely at Deuteronomy 16:1, you will notice the word "celebrate." Their job was to eat, rejoice, remember, be thankful, and celebrate what God had done for them. Only a God of joy would command his people to have a week-long festival every year!

The Feast of Weeks (Labor Day). The second great festival of Israel, found in Deuteronomy 16:9–12, is called the Feast of Weeks. This came during the latter part of the growing season, when they had just begun to take in the first crops. In our calendar year the holiday that marks the end of summer, when we honor the work that has been done, is Labor Day. This Israelite feast was a time to celebrate all the work that had been done and God's provision through the harvest. It is important to note that everyone was called to celebrate this festival: family members, servants, the alien, the orphan, and the widow. No one was to be left out.

The Feast of Tabernacles or Booths (Thanksgiving). The third great feast is described in Deuteronomy 16:13–17. It's called the Feast of Tabernacles or the Feast of Booths. During this feast the people would actually live in tents in order to remember when they lived in the wilderness in portable dwellings. In our day, it might be called the Feast of the Minivans or Campers. This celebration came at the end of the harvest, after the entire harvest had been brought in. In our calendar the time we remember our earliest settlers' thanking God for the harvest is Thanksgiving Day. This is the best modern-day equivalent to remind us of the spirit of the Feast of Booths.

SIGNIFICANT SCRIPTURE

Deuteronomy 16

INTERPRETIVE INSIGHT | Celebrate and Rejoice

There are two words that come up again and again when these feasts and remembrances are commanded in the Pentateuch: *celebrate* and *rejoice*. God is deeply concerned that we grow as people of joy. He wants us, he commands us, to celebrate his great works and amazing provision. In Deuteronomy 16:14 the people are told to "be joyful at your feasts." What a great reminder!

LIFE APPLICATION | The Issue of Inclusiveness

Notice God's concern for including everyone in the celebration (Deuteronomy 16:1–12). The religious leaders, who had no land as their possession, were called to be part of the festival. The immigrants, widows, and orphans were also to be included. They were to be invited, and provision was to be made for them.

God still wants his followers to invite others to join in our celebrations. From church services to backyard holiday BBQs, God wants us to invite others to join in the joy. Our joyous celebrations speak volumes to a world that looks on and wonders if our faith is real. Each time we get ready for some kind of celebration, why not ask ourselves, *Are there people I know who need a little joy in their lives? Whom might I invite to a special church event, a party, or some gathering where Christ-followers are going to be celebrating life?* We can learn to include others in our modern-day festivals and watch what happens as they are swept into the joy of God and his people.

INTERPRETIVE INSIGHT | Set Apart by Joy

Many people think that the Old Testament is a story of a dark, grim God overseeing a scared and somber people. It is not so. God calls his people to be holy. "Be holy as I am holy" means to "be set apart." One of the ways God's people were to be holy, unique, set apart, was to be joyful. The law commands the feasts as reminders, in a sense a kind of training exercise, for joy. Many people have trouble being joyful, but God is ready to help us grow in joy.

If you want to see how serious God is about our growth in joy, look at Deuteronomy 14:22–27. God tells people who can't make it to the formal celebration to plan their own personal festival. God does not want them to miss out on the party! They were called to take their tithe of produce and trade it for silver. Then they were to buy food and drink and resources and throw a party right where they were. Can you believe that's in the Bible? God calls his people to be set apart, and one of the best ways is when our lives reflect the joyful heart of God.

LIFE APPLICATION | Feast Days

How are we doing in the joy category? If we need a little help growing in joy, it might be good to establish a personal feast day once a week. On this day we could eat food we love to eat, listen to music we love to hear, and wear clothes that make us happy. We might even make a point of connecting with people who bring joy to our lives. What a wonderful discipline it would be to establish weekly or monthly days of feasting and joy!

INTERPRETIVE INSIGHT | God's Desire for His Children

The laws about feasts are wonderful. They are designed to free us and train us to become joyful people. God says, "Why don't you get together for a week and just celebrate? Remember my goodness and rejoice in it, revel in it, drink it in!" What is amazing is that God calls his people to this level of celebration many times every year. What a truly joyful God we serve! God wants us to commit ourselves to consistent and passionate celebration of his goodness, because if we keep doing it week after week, month after month, and year after year, there's a good chance that we will become convinced that God is good. As this conviction grows, we will become more joyful people.

ON THE LIGHTER SIDE | Joy-Challenged People

We all know people who are joy-challenged. These are the folks who have the ability to see the cloud inside every silver lining. They have what might be called the "Eeyore Complex." There might be days we need to tell them, "I can't be with you today. It's my feast day today. You'll suck the joy right out of me. I'll be with you tomorrow, but not today. Today I will be walking in joy."

Of course, we would not say it just like that. We would be a little more diplomatic. But the truth is that there should be days we give ourselves space to walk in joy, and this might mean avoiding those who bring our joy-quotient way down. We can encourage them and help them grow in joy another day.

3. "Head-Scratching" Laws

In addition to the laws about generosity and festivals, there are other laws throughout the Pentateuch that can be somewhat confusing. We might call these "head-scratching" laws. These laws seem strange, severe, or sometimes contradictory to the way we envision God.

Through the Pentateuch we read laws that say:

- If you have a rebellious son, you can stone him.

- People can have slaves.

- A husband can write a certificate of divorce to his wife and just send her away if he is displeased with her.

- A woman's vows to God must be cleared through her husband or her father.

- "Eye for eye, tooth for tooth, hand for hand, foot for foot, burn for burn, wound for wound, bruise for bruise" (Exodus 21:24–25).

How do we respond to these laws? In this section we will look at these "head-scratching" laws and put them in a historical context that will help us make sense of them.

SIGNIFICANT SCRIPTURE

Exodus 21:22–24;
Deuteronomy 24:1–4;
Matthew 5

ILLUSTRATION | Eagles, Robins, and Pigeons

In the early years of grade school there are often three reading groups. The teacher always pretends that these groups are all the same, but everyone knows this is not the case. You can tell which group is which by their names. For instance, you might have the eagles as one group—they are the best readers.

HISTORICAL CONTEXT | Starting Where We Are

God has to start where people are. We must remember that at this time in history, the Old Testament had not been written. There were no Scriptures. There was no law of God, and morality was at a rock-bottom level. The world was in relational, spiritual, and moral chaos.

To put it in context, there were all kinds of common practices that would be shocking today. Child sacrifice was practiced and was even part of some religious rituals in pagan worship. Radical revenge and retribution was acceptable. If someone was wronged, they would often take revenge on a whole family rather than just the person who offended them. In some cases, they would take vengeance on a whole city. Cult prostitution existed all over this part of the ancient world, and the people of Israel saw this happening as a normative practice.

As God began to call a community of people to follow him, he started where they were. There was no morality, so he began to introduce beginning steps so they could understand. In a similar way, God still meets each of us where we are and then begins to lead us to where he wants us to be.

Then there might be the robins—these students can read fairly well, but they still need some work. Finally, there are the pigeons—these kids know that they will not be soaring with the eagles.

As we look back at the people of Israel at this time in their history, they are in the pigeon group. Spiritually speaking, they are not eagles or even robins. These are the pigeons. That's what Deuteronomy 1:2 is all about. That is why it took them forty years to take an eleven-day walk. This is not the advance-placement class.

INTERPRETIVE INSIGHT | ## Fully Inspired Yet Written by and for Real People

The Bible is not an example of God dictating heavenly rules for perfect angels. The law was not written by or for angels. Just as Jesus was both fully divine and fully human, the Bible is both fully inspired by God and also written by real human beings. These people had to wrestle, study, and think long and hard about what they wrote.

The Bible was written in a context for real people who had habits, customs, and patterns that were unbelievably destructive. God did not give them everything all at once; they would not have been ready for it. In a sense, God was slowly weaning them away from what was destructive and teaching them the new way of life.

NEW TESTAMENT CONNECTION | ## The Issue of Hardheartedness

A great example of this is found in Mark 10. In this passage Jesus is teaching about the Old Testament law. Mark 10:2–5 says:

> Some Pharisees came and tested him by asking, "Is it lawful for a man to divorce his wife?"
>
> "What did Moses command you?" he replied.
>
> They said, "Moses permitted a man to write a certificate of divorce and send her away."
>
> "It was because your hearts were hard that Moses wrote you this law," Jesus replied.

It is important for us to understand Jesus' interpretation, his understanding, of the Old Testament. He tells them it was because of hardheartedness that Moses permitted divorce. Jesus uses the same word found in those early chapters of Deuteronomy—stubborn, stiff-necked, and hardhearted.

Jesus goes on to teach that God's plan was always for the permanence of marriage. When the Pharisees ask why Moses allowed men to write a certificate of divorce, Jesus basically says, "Because Moses was working with the pigeons. It was a concession to hardheartedness."

You've got to start somewhere, and Moses was taking a first step in getting people to begin taking marriage seriously and to create some accountability. But God's intent was clear in the Old Testament to anybody who looks with an honest, open heart. If we look at Genesis 2, we see that God's plan was for one husband and one wife for an entire lifetime. Jesus was not setting the law aside, he was correctly interpreting it.

INTERPRETIVE INSIGHT | Restraining Common Practices

Often, because God was working with the pigeons back in Moses' day, the laws were given to wean people away from unhealthy and ungodly practices. Because the people's hearts were hard, the strategy was to put limits and restraints around these practices and to help them begin to take steps of change.

For instance, slavery already existed when the Old Testament was written. Moses did not eradicate slavery completely, but a limit of six years was established. Moses also taught that a slave was to be regarded as a brother. Slaves were even allowed to worship with the people of God. Moses said that when a slave was released he should be given gifts to help establish him in freedom. In light of where things were at this time, these were huge steps forward. From where we stand today, they might seem like a step backwards, but in that day, this showed forward progression in human rights and the dignity of people.

When we look at Genesis 1–2, we read that human beings were made in the image of God. That's not compatible with slavery. That's not compatible with God's ultimate dream for the human race. So God kept moving people forward until they finally realized that no one should ever be a slave!

NEW TESTAMENT CONNECTION | An Eye for An Eye

Another example of this concerns Jesus' statement in the Sermon on the Mount, "You have heard that it was said, 'Eye for eye, and tooth for tooth'" (Matthew 5:38). Jesus is quoting from Deuteronomy 19:21 here (also Exodus 21:24; Leviticus 24:20).

In the ancient world, the world in which Moses lived, people with power took whatever vengeance they wanted on somebody who hurt them. If someone was hurt a little bit, they could hurt back a lot. Not only that, but they would even inflict punishment on the next of kin. If they couldn't get at the perpetrator, they would attack and punish a son, daughter, spouse, or even extended family and friends. This disproportionate punishment was common practice. It was considered acceptable.

In light of this, when Moses wrote, "Eye for an eye, tooth for a tooth," it was not encouraging vengeance; it was *limiting it*. This law was intended to restrain vengeance. It taught that evil must be punished, but the punishment must be proportionate, not disproportionate. In light of where people were at this time in history, the people would have realized that this law was given to discourage violence, not to encourage it.

But then Jesus begins talking about loving enemies and offering grace (Matthew 5:39–48). We might wonder: Is Jesus saying that the Old Testament was wrong? The answer is no! Instead, he is taking the limiting power of the law to the next level. He is saying that the time of pigeon responses to enemies is gone, and it is time to soar like an eagle.

NARRATIVE ON LIFE | How Jesus Describes God

Jesus describes the Father in ways that help us know God and love him even more. The God Jesus describes is a God who watches out for sparrows and clothes the lilies of the field. He counts the hairs on our head and searches for a single lost sheep. That's the God Jesus loves, and human beings were so captivated by that picture of God that they sacrificed their lives to follow Jesus.

Many people think there is a gap between the God of the Old Testament and the God Jesus describes. But there is at least one person in history who did not think there was any gap between the God of the Old Testament and the God Jesus knew. That person was Jesus!

We must remember that Jesus is a really smart guy. He read the same Old Testament we read. He was the greatest scholar, interpreter, and teacher of the Old Testament who ever lived. Jesus was convinced that the God he read about in the Old Testament was the same God he describes so beautifully.

PAUSE FOR PRAYER | Closing the Message

As you close the message, consider inviting people to begin praying these words, "May I find in the Old Testament the God that Jesus found." What a wonderful prayer to guide each person as they continue forward in their study of the Old Testament.

Willow Creek Association
Vision, Training, Resources for Prevailing Churches

This resource was created to serve you and to help you in building a local church that prevails!

Since 1992, the Willow Creek Association (WCA) has been linking like-minded, action-oriented churches with each other and with strategic vision, training, and resources. Now a worldwide network of over 6,400 churches from more than ninety denominations, the WCA works to equip Member Churches and others with the tools needed to build prevailing churches. Our desire is to inspire, equip, and encourage Christian leaders to build biblically functioning churches that reach increasing numbers of unchurched people, not just with innovations from Willow Creek Community Church in South Barrington, Illinois, but from any church in the world that has experienced God-given breakthroughs.

WILLOW CREEK CONFERENCES

Each year, thousands of local church leaders, staff and volunteers—from WCA Member Churches and others—attend one of our conferences or training events. Conferences offered on the Willow Creek campus in South Barrington, Illinois, include:

Prevailing Church Conference: Foundational training for staff and volunteers working to build a prevailing local church.

Prevailing Church Workshops: More than fifty strategic, day-long workshops covering seven topic areas that represent key characteristics of a prevailing church; offered twice each year.

Promiseland Conference: Children's ministries; infant through fifth grade.

Student Ministries Conference: Junior and senior high ministries.

Willow Creek Arts Conference: Vision and training for Christian artists using their gifts in the ministries of local churches.

Leadership Summit: Envisioning and equipping Christians with leadership gifts and responsibilities; broadcast live via satellite to eighteen cities across North America.

Contagious Evangelism Conference: Encouragement and training for churches and church leaders who want to be strategic in reaching lost people for Christ.

Small Groups Conference: Exploring how developing a church *of* small groups can play a vital role in developing authentic Christian community that leads to spiritual transformation.

To find out more about WCA conferences, visit our website at www.willowcreek.com.

PREVAILING CHURCH REGIONAL WORKSHOPS

Each year the WCA team leads several, two-day training events in select cities across the United States. Some twenty day-long workshops are offered in topic areas including leadership, next-generation ministries, small groups, arts and worship, evangelism, spiritual gifts, financial stewardship, and spiritual formation. These events make quality training more accessible and affordable to larger groups of staff and volunteers.

To find out more about Prevailing Church Regional Workshops, visit our website at www.willowcreek.com.

WILLOW CREEK RESOURCES™

Churches can look to Willow Creek Resources™ for a trusted channel of ministry tools in areas of leadership, evangelism, spiritual gifts, small groups, drama, contemporary music, financial stewardship, spiritual transformation, and more. For ordering information, call (800) 570-9812 or visit our website at www.willowcreek.com.

WCA MEMBERSHIP

Membership in the Willow Creek Association as well as attendance at WCA Conferences is for churches, ministries, and leaders who hold to a historic, orthodox understanding of biblical Christianity. The annual church membership fee of $249 provides substantial discounts for your entire team on all conferences and Willow Creek Resources, networking opportunities with other outreach-oriented churches, a bimonthly newsletter, a subscription to the *Defining Moments* monthly audio journal for leaders, and more.

To find out more about WCA membership, visit our website at www.willowcreek.com.

WILLOWNET (WWW.WILLOWCREEK.COM)

This Internet resource service provides access to hundreds of Willow Creek messages, drama scripts, songs, videos, and multimedia ideas. The system allows you to sort through these elements and download them for a fee.

Our website also provides detailed information on the Willow Creek Association, Willow Creek Community Church, WCA membership, conferences, training events, resources, and more.

WILLOWCHARTS.COM (WWW.WILLOWCHARTS.COM)

Designed for local church worship leaders and musicians, WillowCharts.com provides online access to hundreds of music charts and chart components, including choir, orchestral, and horn sections, as well as rehearsal tracks and video streaming of Willow Creek Community Church performances.

THE NET (HTTP://STUDENTMINISTRY.WILLOWCREEK.COM)

The NET is an online training and resource center designed by and for student ministry leaders. It provides an inside look at the structure, vision, and mission of prevailing student ministries from around the world. The NET gives leaders access to complete programming elements, including message outlines, dramas, small group questions, and more. An indispensable resource and networking tool for prevailing student ministry leaders!

CONTACT THE WILLOW CREEK ASSOCIATION

If you have comments or questions, or would like to find out more about WCA events or resources, please contact us:

Willow Creek Association
P.O. Box 3188, Barrington, IL 60011-3188
Phone: (800) 570-9812 or (847) 765-0070
Fax (888) 922-0035 or (847) 765-5046
Web: www.willowcreek.com

OLD TESTAMENT CHALLENGE
Discover the Life-Changing Relevance of the Old Testament

Creating a New Community:
Life-Changing Stories from the Pentateuch
John Ortberg with Kevin and Sherry Harney

This dynamic program takes your church on an eye-opening, heart-searching journey through Scripture on three interlocking levels:

- Whole congregation—The major themes of the Old Testament snap into focus during 32 weeks of creative and powerful messages that take your entire congregation through the Old Testament.
- Small groups—Truths taught in corporate worship get reinforced through discussion and relationship. Small groups dig deeper into God's Word and apply it to their daily lives.
- Individual—The Scriptures get up-close-and-personal as each participant is challenged through the *Taking the Old Testament Challenge* individual reading guide.

This threefold approach will drive the truths of Scripture deep into the heart and life of each participant, with applications designed to turn lessons into lifestyles and principles into practice.

From the beginning to the end of our lives, we hunger for community. It's not just how we were created—it's why! God, who enjoys relationship within his being as Father, Son, and Holy Spirit, designed us to reflect his nature through loving and life-giving relationship with him and with each other. Only by participating in God's plan for community can the longing of our hearts be satisfied.

These nine interweaving messages, small group studies, and personal study assignments search the Pentateuch to reveal God's passionate desire for intimacy with his people and among his people. Volume one of the Old Testament Challenge educates through action, not just words. It's an exciting new approach for helping the people in your church move closer to God and to each other.

Old Testament Challenge Vol. 1 kit includes:
- *Church Teacher Resource Message Book* with materials for nine OTC messages
- CD's with nine OTC messages as preached by John Ortberg
- DVD and VHS Video presenting an OTC "vision-casting" message by John Ortberg and four creative video elements for use during OTC messages
- *Small Group Discussion Guide* with nine lessons that follow the OTC sermons
- CD-ROM providing nine PowerPoint presentations for use with each OTC message, Ten FAQ resources for the first ten weeks of the OTC reading guide, and several units of a game, "Are You an Old Testament Expert?"
- *Taking the Old Testament Challenge* reading guide with a forty week (and optional thirty-two week) reading plan.
- *Implementation Guide* for Old Testament Challenge

All materials except audio sermons by John Ortberg also sold separately.

Curriculum Kit
ISBN: 0-310-24891-4

Small Group Discussion Guide
ISBN: 0-310-24893-0

Taking the Old Testament Challenge
ISBN: 0-310-24913-9

DVD Video
ISBN: 0-310-25242-3

PowerPoint® CD-ROM
ISBN: 0-310-25244-X

Implementation Guide
ISBN: 0-310-24939-2

VHS Video
ISBN: 0-310-252431

Pick up a copy today at your favorite bookstore!

ZONDERVAN™
GRAND RAPIDS, MICHIGAN 49530 USA
WWW.ZONDERVAN.COM